Travelers' Self Care Manual

Travelers' Self Care Manual

By William W. Forgey, M.D.

A self help guide to emergency medical treatment for the traveler.

Dr. Forgey is a member, Medical Advisory Board, International Association for Medical Assistance to Travelers (IAMAT), Toronto, Canada; Assistant Clinical Professor of Family Medicine, Indiana University, Northwest Campus, Gary, Indiana; Chairman, Department of Family Practice, St. Mary Mercy Hospital Center of Gary and Hobart, Indiana; and Medical Director, Herchmer Medical Consultants, Merrillville, Indiana.

ICS BOOKS, INC.
Merrillville, Indiana

Travelers' Self Care Manual
Copyright © 1990 by William W. Forgey, M.D.

10 9 8 7 6 5 4 3 2 1

Dedication

I fondly dedicate this book to the physician whom I consider my greatest instructor, Robert M. Seibel, M.D. in Nashville, Indiana. Thanks Bob, for getting me started!

Library of Congress Cataloging-in-Publication Data

Forgey, William W., 1942-
    Travelers' self care manual / by William W. Forgey ; illustrations
by Scott Power.
        p.   cm.
    Includes index.
    ISBN 0-934802-63-7 : $6.95
    1. Travel--Health aspects--Handbooks, manuals, etc. 2. First aid
in illness and injury--Handbooks, manuals, etc. 3. Self-care.
Health-Handbooks, manuals, etc.   I. Title.
    RC88.9.T76F67   1990
    616.02'52--dc20   90-4970
                                                      Rev. CIP

ABOUT THE AUTHOR

Dr. Forgey is Assistant Clinical Professor of Family Medicine, Indiana University School of Medicine, Northwest Indiana Campus; a member of the Medical Advisory Board of the International Association for Medical Assistance to Travelers (IAMAT), Toronto, Canada; Department Chairman, Family Practice, St. Mary Mercy Medical Center at Gary and Hobart, Indiana; Trustee of the Wilderness Education Association, Saranac Lake, New York; Adjunct Faculty Member, Western Illinois University, College of Health, Physical Education & Recreation, Macomb, Illinois; Adjunct Faculty Member, Slippery Rock University, Department of Parks & Recreation, Slippery Rock, Pennsylvania; and currently is in private practice in Merrillville, Indiana.

Prior to going to medical school he held the rank of Captain, Infantry, and had over two years of service in the former Republic of Vietnam.

He is an Active Member of the American Medical Writers Association and the Outdoor Writers Association of America. A Fellow of the Explorer's Club, New York City, Dr. Forgey is also an Associate Member of the Univeristy Association for Emergency Medicine.

Other publications by Dr. Forgey include *Wilderness Medicine* (1979, 2d Ed 1983, 3rd Ed 1987), *Hypothermia* (1985), *Campfire Stories* (1985), *Basic Essentials of Outdoor First Aid* (1989), *Campfire Tales* (1989), and *The Travelers' Medical Resource* (1990) all published by ICS Books. Dr. Forgey contributed to the current edition of the Field Book, published by the Boy Scouts of America. He is a consultant for many outdoor programs, camps, and expeditions.

Table of Contents

Chapter 1

Trauma

WOUND CARE

The most common minor injuries while traveling will be sun burn, friction blisters, and twisted ankles and knees. Although the first two are certainly preventable, they will never-the-less still occur to even the most experienced traveler.

Friction Blisters

A relatively new and easily obtainable substance has revolutionized the prevention and care of friction blisters. The substance is Spenco 2nd Skin, available at most athletic supply and drug stores. Made from an inert, breathable gel consisting of 4% polyethylene oxide and 96% water, it has the feel and consistency of cold jello. It comes in various sized sterile sheets, sealed in water-tight packages. It is very cool to the touch, in fact large sheets are sold to cover infants to

reduce a fever. It has three valuable properties
that make it so useful. One, it will remove all
friction between two moving surfaces (hence its
use in prevention) and two, it cleans and deodor-
izes wounds by absorbing blood, serum, or pus.
Three, its cooling effect is very soothing, which
aids in pain relief.

After opening the sealed package, you will
find the Spenco 2nd Skin sandwiched between
two sheets of cellophane. Remove the cellophane
from the side which will be applied to the wound
or hot spot. It must be secured to the wound and
for that purpose the same company produces an
adhesive knit bandage.

For treatment of a hot spot, remove the cellophane from one side and apply this gooey side
against the wound, securing it with the knit bandaging. If a friction blister has developed, it will
have to be lanced. Cleanse with soap or surgical
scrub and open along an edge with a clean, thin
blade. After expressing the fluid, apply a fully
stripped piece of 2nd Skin. This is easiest done
by removing the cellophane from one side, then
apply it to the wound. Once on the skin surface,
remove the cellophane from the top surface. Over
this you will need to place the adhesive knit. The
bandage must be kept moist with clean water.
Applied through the adhesive knit, routine moist-
ening will allow the same bandage to be used for
days or until the wound is healed.

Thermal Burns

Sun burns have ruined more vacations than
any other single injury. These burns are generally
first degree (with red, painful skin) or second
degree (with red, blistered, painful skin), and
can even result in shock from fluid loss and pain.
The victim will feel relief with cool compresses

(or even soaked sheets), but care must be taken to avoid too much cooling or they may become hypothermic. Various ointments have been developed to help with first and second degree burns, such as topical anesthetics (which are usually formulations of dibucaine) and various antispetic combinations. Dibucaine can be sensitizing and might result in an allergic reaction or increased skin rash, but generally works quite well.

The Spenco 2nd Skin mentioned above also works quite well for burn treatment, but will seldom be available in sheets large enough to treat sun burn.

Pain medication should be provided. Early inflammation will respond to topical steroids, but the major effort should be to provide pain relief and moisturizing creams. Aloe vera ointment also works quite well in treating minor, first degree burns.

Thermal burns can also be first and second degree, but may also result in charred tissue, or third degree burns. As soon as possible remove the source of the burn—quick immersion into cool water will help eliminate additional heat from scalding water or burning fuels and clothing. Or otherwise suffocate the flames with clothing, sand, etc.

The field treatment of burns has also been revolutionized by the development of Spenco 2nd Skin. It is the perfect substance to use on 1st, 2nd, or 3rd degree burns. Its cooling effect relieves pain, while its sterile covering absorbs fluid easily from the wound. If applied to a charred 3rd degree burn, it provides a sterile cover that does not have to be changed. When the patient arrives at a hospital, it can easily be removed in a whirlpool bath.

Burn patients can generally be self managed

quite well if the wounds are not worse than 2nd degree and as long as they do not cover more than 15% of the body surface area of an adult (10% of a child). Burns more extensive than this, and burns which involve the face or include more than one joint of the hand, are best treated professionally. The first aid treatment will be as above, but additionally, treat for shock and try to find professional help.

Lacerations

Direct pressure is the best method of stopping bleeding—in fact pressure alone can stop bleeding from amputated limbs! When the accident first occurs, you may even need to use your bare hand to stem the flow of blood. This direct pressure may have to be applied 5, 10, even 30 minutes or longer. Apply it as long as it takes! With the blood stopped, even if only with your hand, and the victim on the ground in the shock treatment position, the actual emergency is over. The victim's life has been saved. And you have bought the time to gather together various items you need to perform the definitive job of caring for this wound. You have also treated for psychogenic shock—the shock of "fear". For obviously someone knows what to do: they have taken charge, they have stopped the bleeding, they are giving orders to gather materials together. This shock caused by fear is more of a problem than that caused by the loss of blood.

In the first aid management of this wound, the next step is simply bandaging and then transporting the victim to professional medical care. Further care of a wound takes the practitioner beyond the first aid phase. It is generally best to seek professional help for aggressive wound cleansing and closure technique. However, after thorough cleansing, most wounds can be closed with strips of tape, such as butterfly closures, or more sophisticated tape closures (Steri-Strips, Cover-Strips). A complete description of wound closure techniques can be found in *Wilderness Medicine*.

Abrasions

An abrasion is the loss of surface skin due to a scraping injury. The best treatment is cleansing with Hibiclens surgical scrub, application of triple antibiotic ointment, and the use of Spenco 2nd Skin with Adhesive Knit Bandage—all components of the Travel Medical Kit. This type of wound oozes profusely, but the above bandaging allows rapid healing, excellent protection, and considerable pain relief. Avoid the use of alcohol on these wounds as it tends to damage the tissue, to say nothing of causing excessive pain. Lacking first aid supplies, cleanse gently with mild detergent and protect from dirt, bugs, etc., the best that you can. Tetanus immunization should have been received within 10 years.

Puncture Wounds

Allow puncture wounds to bleed, thus hoping to effect an automatic irrigation of bacteria from the wound. If available, apply suction with the Extractor (venom suction device) immediately and continue the vacuum for 20 to 30 minutes. The Extractor is recommended for inclusion in a Travel Medical Kit under certain circumstances as mentioned in that section. Cleanse the wound area with surgical scrub—or soapy water—and apply triple antibiotic ointment to the surrounding skin surface. Do not tape shut, but rather start warm compress applications for 20 minutes, every 2 hours for the next 2 days.

These soaks should be as warm as the patient can tolerate without danger of burning the skin. Larger pieces of cloth work best—such as undershirts—as they hold the heat longer. If sterile items are in short supply, they need not be used on this type of wound. Use clean clothes, or boil such items and allow to cool and dry before use. Tetanus immunization should be within 5 years for dirty injuries such as puncture wounds. Red coloration of the skin, extending more than $1/4$th inch from the wound edge could indicate a wound infection. If this develops, start the patient on oral antibiotics such as the doxycycline 100 mg twice daily.

Shock Treatment

Injury care can be broken into chronological phases. The first phase consists of SAVING THE VICTIM'S LIFE—by stopping the bleeding and treating for shock. Even if the victim is not bleeding, you will want to treat for shock. Shock has many fancy medical definitions, but on the bottom line it amounts to an inadequate oxygenated blood supply getting to the head. Lay the patient down, elevate feet above the head, and provide protection from the environment—from both the ground and the atmosphere. Grab anything which you can find for this at first—use jackets, newspapers, pieces of cardboard, or whatever.

Patients with head injuries are best allowed to have slight head elevation, unless concern for a neck injury exists. It is essential to immobilize the patient with an injured neck to prevent spinal cord damage.

Wound Infection

The formation of slight red discoloration around a wound edge is generally part of the healing process. However, an excessive spread of this red discoloration—say 1/4th of an inch beyond the wound margin—usually indicates that an infection is forming.

The best treatment is to allow this wound to gape open (remove tape closures, etc., if they have been applied). Apply warm, wet soaks for fifteen to twenty minutes every two hours to promote drainage and increase circulation in the area to aid the body in defending itself against the infection.

If antibiotics are available, this is the time to use them. From the recommended prescription medical kit use the doxycycline 100 mg, giving one tablet twice daily. Your physician may recommend an alternate antibiotic which should then be included in your medical kit, with the instructions he has given you also recorded in the instruction section provided at the end of this section.

Splinter Removal

Prepare the wound with Hibiclens surgical scrub, soapy water, or other cleansing solution that does not discolor the skin. Minute splinters are hard enough to see without discoloring the skin and disguising them even more. If the splinter is shallow, or the point buried, use a needle or thin knife blade to tease the tissue over the splinter to remove this top layer. The splinter can then be pried up or more easily grasped with the tweezers or splinter forceps.

Figure 1
Hold splinter forceps
or tweezer parallel to
the skin surface and
grasp the splinter only
after obtaining an ade-
quate exposure by un-
roofing it adequately.

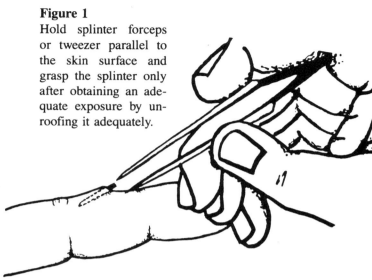

It is best to be aggressive in removing this top
layer of skin and obtaining a substantial bite on the
splinter with the tweezers, rather than nibbling off
the end while making futile attempts to remove it
due to inadequate exposure. When using the splinter forceps, grasp the instrument between the
thumb and forefinger, resting the instrument on the
middle finger and further resting the entire hand
against the victim's skin, if necessary, to prevent
tremor. Approach the splinter from the side, if
exposed, grasping it as low as possible. Remove
it along the same direction as its entry path. Apply triple antibiotic afterwards.

Tetanus immunization should be current
within 10 years, or if a dirty wound, within 5
years. If the wound was dirty, scrub afterwards
with Hibiclens or soapy water. If deep, treat as
indicated above under PUNCTURE WOUND
with hot soaks and antibiotic as indicated.

Chapter 2

Eye, Ear, Nose, Mouth

No portion of our general well being affects us as much as our five senses, and four of them relate to proper function of the above organs.

Eye

Foreign bodies, abrasions, and infections (conjunctivitis) are the most frequently encountered eye problems. Therapy for these problems is virtually the same, except that it is very important to remove any foreign body that may be present.

Foreign Body

A calm, careful examination is necessary to adequately examine the eye for a foreign body.

Very carefully shine a small light at the cornea (the surface of the eye lying over the pupil and iris) from one side to see if a minute speck becomes visible. By moving the light back and forth, one might see movement of a shadow on the iris of the eye and thus confirm the presence of a foreign body. A shadow that consistently stays put with blinking is probably a foreign body.

In making the foreign body examination, also be sure to check under the eyelids. Evert the upper lid over a Q-tip stick, thus examining not only the eyeball, but also the under-surface of the eyelid. See figure 2. This surface may be gently brushed with the cotton applicator to eliminate minute particles. Always use a fresh Q-tip when touching the eye or eyelid each additional time.

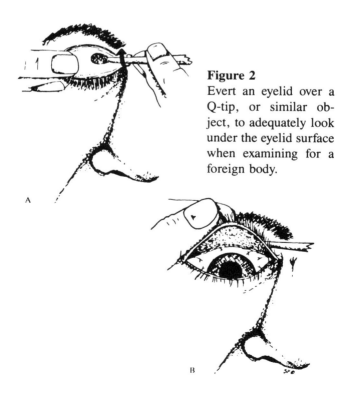

Figure 2
Evert an eyelid over a Q-tip, or similar object, to adequately look under the eyelid surface when examining for a foreign body.

When a foreign body has been found, it can frequently be rinsed off with running water. One method is for the victim to hold their face under water and blink their eyes. Sometimes it can be easily prodded off with the edge of a clean cloth.

Leave stubborn foreign bodies for removal by a physician in all but the most desperate circumstances. The patient should be evacuated to a physician at once, if at all possible. If you are stuck without professional help and have a difficult time removing an obvious foreign body from the surface of the cornea, a wait of two to three days may allow the cornea to ulcerate slightly so that removal by gentle prodding with a Q-tip handle may be *much* easier. Deeply lodged foreign bodies will have to be left for surgical removal.

Patching the eye will help alleviate pain. Patch techniques for the eye must allow for gentle closure of the eyelid and retard blinking activity. Generally both eyes must be patched for this to succeed. Simple strips of tape holding the eyelids shut may suffice. In case of trauma, a ring of cloth may be constructed to pad the eye without pressure over the eyeball. A simple eye patch with over-size gauze or cloth may work fine, as the bone of the orbital rim around the eye acts to protect the eyeball which is recessed. Try to avoid patching both eyes, except at times when the patient is resting. If eye drops are available, they can provide some relief, but antibiotic drops are prescription medications. Seek professional help for any eye condition as soon as possible.

Eye Abrasion

Carefully examine the eye surface to insure that no foreign body is present. Check under the eyelids as indicated above. An abrasion on the eye will feel like a foreign body is present. Treat

with soothing eye drops if available. Patch for
comfort as indicated above.

Eye infection

An infection of the eye will be heralded by a
scratchy feeling, almost indistinguishable from a
foreign body in the eye. The sclera, or white of
the eye, will be pink or red. Generally the eye
will be matted shut in the morning with pus or
granular matter.

Rinse with clean water frequently during the
day. Eye infections such as bacterial conjunctivitis, the most common infection, are self limiting
and will generally clear themselves within two
weeks. They can become much worse, however,
so medical attention should be sought. Do not
patch, but protect the eyes from sunlight. When
one eye is infected, treat both eyes as the infection spreads easily to the non-infected eye.

Eye infections should be treated with a prescription antibiotic such as Tobrex ophthalmic
ointment. If nasal congestion is also present,
treatment with a decongestant, such as Actifed, is
quite appropriate.

Styes

Many persons form styes upon exposure to
sun. This can be prevented by wearing sunglasses, wide brimmed hats, or other eye protection that prevents direct and reflected sun
exposure to the eye lids.

Treatment is with warm compresses, antibiotic eye ointment. Frequently, oral antibiotics are
prescribed for this condition.

Sun and Snow Blindness

This severely painful condition is primarily
caused by ultraviolet B rays of the sun which are

considerably reflected by snow (85%), water (10–100%), and sand (17%). Thin cloud layers allow the transmission of this wavelength, while filtering out infra-red (heat) rays of the sun. Thus, it is possible on a rather cool, overcast day under bright snow conditions to become sunburned or snow blind.

Properly approved (ANSI) sunglasses will block 99.8% of the ultraviolet B wavelength. Suitable glasses should be tagged as meeting these standards[1]

In 1989 the Food and Drug Administration announced a new system of labeling sunglasses based on their effectiveness in removing both the short-wave UVB and the longer wave and more penetrating UVA. Sunglasses will be in three categories:

1. Cosmetic. They will block at least 70 percent of the UVB and 20 percent of the UVA radiation. Cosmetic sunglasses will be recommended for shopping or other "around town" activities away from harsh sunlight.

2. General Purpose. These will block from 60 percent to 92 percent of visible light and range in shade from medium to dark. They keep out at least 95 percent of UVB and at least 60 percent of UVA rays. These are recommended for a sunny environment and activities such as boating, driving, flying, or hiking.

[1]The American National Standards Institute, or ANSI, establishes specifications for many manufactured products.

3. Special Purpose. This model will block
   at least 97 percent of the visible light and
   at least 99 percent of UVB and 60 percent UVA radiation. They are recommended for very bright environments
   such as tropical beaches or snowy ski
   slopes.

The fit of sunglasses is extremely important.
Side protection must be sought in conditions of
reflective light. Slippage of sunglasses by as little
as one fourth of an inch can increase UV exposure by 20%.

A suitable retention strap must be worn, as I
recently once again learned while rafting on the
Green River in Colorado. And for those of us
who must learn these things more than once, a
second pair of glasses—particularly if prescription lenses are worn—is essential. Lacking sunglasses, any field expedient method of
eliminating glare, such a slit glasses made from
wood or any material at hand, to include the
ubiquitous bandana, will help. An important aspect of sun blindness is the delayed onset of
symptoms. The pain and loss of vision may not
be evident until after damaging exposure has
been sustained.

Sun blindness is a self limiting affliction.
However, not only is the actual loss of vision a
problem, but so is the terrible pain, usually described as feeling like red hot pokers were mas-
saging the eye sockets. Lacking any first aid
supplies, the treatment would be gentle eye patch
and the application of cold packs as needed for
pain relief. Generally both eyes are equally affected with a virtual total loss of vision. If there
is partial sight, then patching the most affected
eye may be practical. Otherwise, rest both eyes.

The prescription Pontocaine ophthalmic ointment will help ease the pain, but long term use can delay eye surface healing. Oral pain medication will be of help and should be used. The severe pain can last from hours to several days. In case a drainage of pus, or crusting of the eyelids occurs, start antibiotic ophthalmic ointment applications as indicated in the section on conjunctivitis. Further information on sun injury may be found on page 2.

Ear

The development of ear pain is a sure way to ruin a trip. Pain in the ear can be due to a number of causes. Air squeeze, or barotrauma, or a history of injury will be an obvious source of pain. Most ear pain is due to an *otitis media* or infection behind the ear drum (tympanic membrane), *otitis externa* or infection in the outer ear canal (auditory canal), or due to infection elsewhere (generally a dental infection, infected tonsil, or lymph node in the neck near the ear). Allergy can result in pressure behind the ear drum and is also a common source of ear pain.

Air Squeeze

Air squeeze, or barotrauma, can result in a painful ear. Rapid ascents or descents in vehicles and airplanes can cause significant pain from pressure or vacuum in the middle ear. This is particularly true if the passenger is suffering from head congestion. Congestion can lead to blockage of the eustachian tube. Failure to equilibrate pressure through this tube between the middle ear and the throat—and, thus, the outside world—can result in damage to the ear drum.

The descent on an airplane is generally the time most likely to cause ear pain for an adult or, especially, a child. Bottle or breast feeding an infant or young child may help alleviate the pressure differential between the middle ear and the ambient pressure.

Try to equalize this pressure by pinching the nose shut and gently increasing the pressure in your mouth and throat against closed lips. This will generally clear the eustachian tube and relieve the air squeeze on the ear drum. Do not over-do this; that can also be painful.

Head congestion should be vigorously treated to prevent eustachian tube blockage. Take a decongestant, such as Actifed. Drink larger amounts of fluid than normal to over hydrate. This tends to thin mucous secretions and can result in less clogging of both sinus cavities and the eustachian tube. While I do not recommend nasal sprays for long-term application, before a flight use a long acting nasal spray, such as Afrin (2 sprays 1 hour before flight time). Persons using such products longer than 3 days are apt to suffer from a rebound congestion when ceasing their use. However, these drops will help to shrink the membranes around the eustachian tube opening in the pharynx and decrease mucous secretion quite effectively. The chance of eustachian tube blockage and experiencing barotrauma, or ear pressure squeeze, is thus greatly reduced.

If barotrauma results in ear drum rupture, the pain should instantly cease. There may be bloody drainage from the ear canal. Do not place drops in the ear canal, but drainage can be gently wiped away or frequently changed cotton plugs used to catch the bloody fluid. Seek medical attention as soon as possible.

Ear Infections
A simple physical examination and a little

additional medical history will readily (and generally accurately) distinguish the difference between an *otitis media* or *otitis externa*, and sources of pain beyond the ear. Pushing on the knob at the front of the ear (the tragus) or pulling on the ear lobe will elicit pain with an *otitis externa*. This will not hurt if the patient has *otitis media*. The history of head congestion also favors *otitis media*.

Otitis Externa—Outer Ear Infection

This infection of the auditory canal is commonly called "swimmer's ear". The external auditory canal generally becomes inflamed from conditions of high humidity, accumulation of ear wax, or contact with contaminated water. Scratching the ear after itching the nose or scratching elsewhere may also be a source of this common infection.

Prevent cold air from blowing against the ear. Warm packs against the ear or instilling comfortably warm sweet oil, or even clean cooking oil, can help. Provide pain medication. Obtain professional help if the patient develops a fever, the pain becomes severe, or lymph nodes or adjacent neck tissues start swelling. Significant tissue swelling will require antibiotic treatment such as doxycycline 100 mg twice daily. Non-prescription ear drops will not clear infections, but can help with pain and local irritation.

Otitis media—Middle Ear Infection

This condition will present in a person who has sinus congestion and possibly drainage from allergy or infection. The ear pain can be excruciating. Fever will frequently be intermittent, normal at one moment and over 103° F at other times. Fever indicates bacterial infection of the fluid trapped behind the ear drum. If the ear drum ruptures, the pain will cease immediately and the fever will drop. This drainage allows the body to cure the infection, but will result in at least temporary damage to the ear drum and decreased hearing until it heals.

Treatment will consist of providing decongestant, pain medication and oral antibiotic such as the doxycycline. An ideal decongestant is Actifed, 1 tablet 4 times daily. Give oral pain medication.

Foreign body in the Ear

These are generally of three types. Accumulation of wax plugs (cerumen), foreign objects, and living insects. Wax plugs can usually be softened with a warmed oil. This may have to be placed in the ear canal repeatedly over many days. Irrigating with room temperature water may be attempted with a bulb syringe. If a wax plugged ear becomes painful, treat as indicated in the section on *otitis externa*.

Figure 3
Bulb syringe for irrigating wounds, ear, or eye as described in the text.

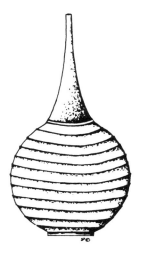

The danger in trying to remove inanimate objects is the tendency to shove them further into the ear canal or to damage the delicate ear canal lining, thus adding bleeding to your troubles. Of course, rupturing the ear drum by shoving against it would be a real unnecessary disaster. Attempt to grasp a foreign body with a pair of tweezers if you can visualize it. Do not poke blindly with anything. Irrigation may be attempted as indicated above.

A method of aiding in the management of insects in the ear canal is to drown the bug with cooking or other oil, then attempt removal. Oil seems to kill bugs quicker than water. The less struggle, the less chance for stinging, biting, or other trauma to the delicate ear canal and ear drum. Tilt the ear downward, thus hoping to slide the dead bug towards the entrance where it can be grappled. Shining a light at the ear to coax a bug out is probably futile.

Nose Bleed (Epistaxis)

If nose bleeding is caused from a contusion to the nose, the bleeding is usually self limited. Bleeding that starts without trauma is generally more difficult to stop. Most bleeding is from small arteries located near the front of the nose partition, or nasal septum.

The best treatment is direct pressure. Have the victim squeeze the nose between his fingers for ten minutes by the clock (a very long time when there is no clock to watch), in the location as illustrated in figure 4. If this fails, squeeze another ten minutes. Do not blow the nose for this will dislodge clots and start the bleeding all over again.

If the bleeding is severe, have the victim sit up to prevent choking on blood and to aid in the

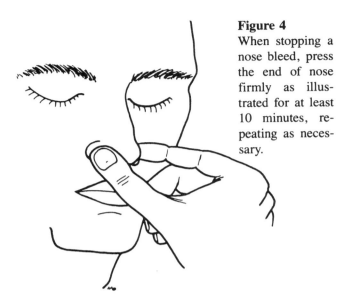

Figure 4
When stopping a nose bleed, press the end of nose firmly as illustrated for at least 10 minutes, repeating as necessary.

reduction of the blood pressure in the nose. Cold compresses do little good. The field treatment of nose fractures and dislocations and advanced techniques of dealing with severe bloody noses are described in my book *Wilderness Medicine*.

Dental Pain, Lost Filling, and Trauma

Cavities may be identified by visual examination of the mouth in most cases. Dry the tooth and try to clean out any cavity found. For years oil of cloves, or eugenol, has been used to deaden dental pain. A daub of topical anesthetic such as 1% dibucaine ointment will also help deaden dental pain. Avoid trying to apply an aspirin directly to a painful tooth, it will only make a worse mess of things.

When you examine a traumatized mouth and find a tooth that is rotated, or dislocated in any direction, do not push the tooth back into place. Further movement may disrupt the tooth's blood and nerve supply. If the tooth is at all secure, leave it alone. The musculature of the lips and tongue will generally gently push the tooth back into place and keep it there.

A broken tooth with that is bleeding or that displays an exposed pink substance, will also have exposed the nerve. This tooth will need protection with eugenol as indicated above. This is a dental emergency that should be treated by a dentist immediately.

If a tooth is knocked out, replace it into the socket immediately. If this cannot be done, have the victim hold the tooth under their tongue or in their lower lip until it can be implanted. In any case hours is a matter of great importance. A tooth left out too long will be rejected by the body as a foreign substance. All of the above problems will mean that a soft diet and avoidance of chewing with the affected tooth for many days will be necessary. Persons suffering dental trauma should be taken to a dentist as soon as possible.

Chapter 3

Abdominal Pain

Even with years of clinical experience and unlimited laboratory and x-ray facilities, abdominal pain can be a diagnostic dilemma. For the traveler confronted with abdominal pain, the major decision is concerning the seriousness of the problem—should professional help be obtained or can the condition be safely self-medicated.

Diagnosis is frequently discerned by the type of pain, location, cause, fever—all from the history—as well as certain aspects of the physical exam and the clinical course that develops.

Burning—upper part of the stomach in the middle (mid-epigastrium) is probably **GASTRITIS**. If allowed to persist this can develop into an **ULCER**—which is a crater eaten into the stom-

TABLE 1
Symptoms and Signs of Abdominal Pathology

	Burning	Nausea	Food Related	Diarrhea	Fever
Gastritis/ulcer	xx	x	xx		
Pancreatitis	xx	x	x		x
Hiatal Hernia	xx		x		
Gall Bladder		xx	xx		(x)
Appendicitis		x			x
Gastro-enteriti		xx		xx	x
Diverticulitis				xx	x
Hepatitis		xx	x		x
Food Poisoning		xx	xx	xx	x

ach wall. Severe persistent mid-epigastric pain, that is frequently burning in nature, can be **PANCREATITIS**. This is a serious problem, but rare. Alcohol consumption can cause pancreatitis, as well as gastritis and ulcer formation. Alcohol must be avoided if pain in this area develops. Reflux of stomach acid up the esophagus, sometimes caused by a **HIATAL HERNIA**, will cause the same symptoms. Treatment for all of the above is aggressive antacid therapy. These conditions can be made worse with spicy food, tomato products, and other foods high in acid content and these should be avoided. Avoid any medication that contains aspirin or ibuprofen, but Tylenol (acetaminophen) containing products are all right. Acid suppression medication such as Tagamet, Zantac, Axid, or Pepcid can help greatly, but these medications can make the user more vulnerable to traveler's diarrhea and other infectious disease from which normal or high stomach acid would otherwise help provide protection. A safer medication for persons afflicted with frequent heart burn, not responsive to antacids, would be Carafate taken 1 gram 4 times daily. This prescription drug should be added to the traveler's medical kit, if necessary.

Nausea with pain in the patient's right upper quadrant may be from a **GALL BLADDER** problem. This discomfort is made worse with eating—sometimes even smelling—fatty foods. While cream would initially help the pain of gastritis or ulcer, it would cause an immediate increase in symptoms if the gall bladder is involved. Part of the treatment is avoidance of fatty foods. Nausea can be treated with the meclizine 25 mg tablets from the non-prescription kit, but would respond much better to the Atarax 25 mg given every 4 to 6 hours from the prescription kit. There is no burning sensation with gall bladder pain. A safe medication would be the use of Tylenol #3. The development of a fever is an important sign which could indicate an infection in an obstructed gall bladder. An infection of the gall bladder is a surgical emergency. Treat the nausea and pain as indicated. Offer as much fluid as tolerated. Gall bladder disease is most common in overweight people in their 40's. It is more common in women.

The possibility of **APPENDICITIS** is a major concern as it can occur in any age group, and that includes even healthy travelers. It is fortunately rare. While surgery is the treatment of choice, probably as many as 70% of people not treated with surgery can survive this disaster, even more with appropriate IV therapy. The classic presentation of this illness is a vague feeling of discomfort around the umbilicus (navel). Temperature may be a low grade fever, 99.6 to 100.6 at first. Within a matter of hours the discomfort turns to pain and localizes in the right lower quadrant, most frequently on a point 1/3 of the way between the navel and the very top of the right pelvic bone (anterior-superior iliac spine), the so-called Mc Burney's point (see figure 5). This pain syndrome can be evaluated by asking two questions: Where did you first start hurting? (belly button); Now where do you hurt? (right lower quadrant as described). Those answers give an 80% probability of appendicitis. Obtain professional help when abdominal pain persists longer than 12 hours, regardless of suspected cause.

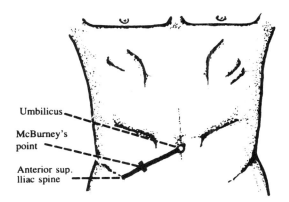

Figure 5
The location of McBurney's Point, the location of maximum pain in classic appendicitis.

Bladder Infection

The symptoms of a bladder infection are the urge to urinate frequently, burning upon urination, small amounts of urine being voided with each attempt, and discomfort in the suprapublic region, the lowest area of the abdomen. Frequently the victim has fever with its attendant chills and muscle ache. Cloudiness and discoloration of the urine is generally not of help in the diagnosis of bladder infections. The ideal treatment is with prescription antibiotics such as the Bactrim DS or doxycycline 100 mg, one tablet twice daily.

Vomiting

Nausea and vomiting are frequently caused by infections known as gastroenteritis. Many times these are viral so that antibiotics are of no value. These infections will usually resolve without treatment in 24 to 48 hours. Fever seldom is high, but may briefly be high in some cases. Fever should not persist above 100 degrees longer than 12 hours. Treatment may be with meclizine, or Atarax—as indicated in the discussions of those drugs—for symptomatic relief. Vomiting without diarrhea will not require the use of an antibiotic. If the vomiting is caused from severe illness, such as an ear infection, then use of antibiotic to treat the underlying cause is justified.

Diarrhea

Pepto Bismol liquid, taken 1 oz every 30 minutes for eight doses, has been shown to decreased the rate of stooling by half. Adsorbents such as kaolin and pectin give stools more consistency, but do not decrease the frequency, abdominal cramping, or length of affliction. A new adsorbent, Diasorb, has ten times the adsorption capability of kaolin and shows great promise in safely treating diarrhea. It is non-prescription and is available in liquid and tablet formulation at most drug stores in the United States. It should be perfectly safe for consumption by women at any stage of pregnancy. Replacement of fluid loss is the important aspect of diarrhea treatment. Carbonated water found in most developing countries is generally considered safe. Water consumed must be either heated to boiling or be bottled water from a reputable source. More than water is lost with the diarrhea. Various minerals are also excreted in large amounts, notably sodium and potassium. The patient must receive adequate fluid replacement, equaling fluid loss plus about 2 quarts per day.

The Centers for Disease Control has developed an oral replacement cocktail to replace the water and mineral (electrolyte) losses of profound diarrhea. (See table 2.)

Throughout the world UNICEF and WHO (World Health Organization) distribute an electrolyte replacement product called Oralyte. It must be reconstituted with adequately purified water.

Anti-motility agents rapidly stop the symptoms of diarrhea. Products such as paregoric, Lomotil, and Imodium are widely used in the treatment of diarrhea. Imodium, in liquid form, was made an non-prescription drug in the United States in mid-1988, while the capsules were made non-prescription in 1989. The adult dose of Imodium is two 2 mg capsules at the onset of treatment, followed by 1 capsule with each loose stool up to a maximum of 8 capsules a day. The use of anti-motility agents should be restricted to urgent situations, such as long bus rides or trips without toilet facilities, impending dehydration,

---

TABLE 2
The CDC Oral Fluid Replacement Cocktail

Prepare two separate glasses of the following:
Glass 1) Orange, apple or other fruit juice rich in potassium)
8 ounces

Honey or corn syrup (glucose necessary for absorption of essential salts)
1/2 teaspoon

Salt, table (source of sodium and chloride)
1 pinch

Glass 2) Water (carbonated or boiled)
8 ounces

Soda, baking (sodium bicarbonate)
1/4 teaspoon

Drink alternately from each glass. Supplement with carbonated beverages or water and tea made with boiled or carbonated water as desired. Avoid solid foods and milk until recovery.

---

attendance at meetings that cannot be cancelled, and the like.

Antibiotic treatment that has been proven effective is the use of doxycycline 100 mg, one tablet twice daily—if this medication was not being taken as a preventative. Bactrim DS (Septra DS), one tablet twice daily—or in the event of sulfa allergy, trimethoprim alone, 200 mg taken twice daily. Three days of treatment is recommended, although 2 days may be sufficient. Nausea and vomiting without diarrhea should not be treated with antibiotics. Erythromycin has been advocated for treatment of travelers' diarrhea. An antibiotic that has been proven quite effective in treatment is Cipro (ciprofloxacin), taken 500 mg twice daily for three to four days. While more effective in a controlled study than Bactrim, its cost is much higher (Cipro costs almost $2.50 per tablet).

Motion Sickness

Motion induced nausea and vomiting can be minimized by various techniques.

When traveling by a vehicle, it helps to ride in the portion less subjected to movement. For a bus this would be between the front and rear wheels. That location, incidentally, is not exactly in the middle of the bus, but somewhat forward of the apparent middle of the coach. In a car, the front seat is far preferable to the rear seat. On a plane, position yourself at the location of the center wings. Generally this obstructs your view. The ideal seat would also be the one next to the wing emergency exit. The safest location in the plane is in the back row of seats towards the trail of the aircraft, but motion problems would be greatly magnified. On a ship, locate yourself as near the center of the ship as possible. However, these are not the choicest rooms for view or amenities.

Activity can also minimize motion problems. Avoid reading. Choose a focal point for your gaze that is as near the horizon as possible. When in a car, look at houses or scenery in the distance. Aboard a plane, look at distant cloud formations. At night, or when a white out blocks outside viewing, focus your attention as far up the aisle as possible. On a ship, stare at the horizon, or as far along the ship deck as you can.

Several medications are available over the counter for control of nausea. Dramamine, Bonine, and Marezine are the most commonly available. Dramamine also has a liquid formulation. A curious fact is the Bonine (meclizine 25 mg), one tablet daily is an non-prescription product to prevent motion sickness, while Antivert (meclizine 25 mg), up to one tablet three times daily, is a prescription required dose to prevent or treat vertigo or motion sickness. There tends to be minimal drowsiness or other side effects when using the above medications.

Transderm Scop, a patch containing scopolamine, has been developed for prevention of motion sickness, but this requires a prescription. Each patch may be worn behind the ear for 3 days. It is fairly expensive, but also very effective and well worth the cost if you are prone to this malady. There tends to be a higher frequency of side effects with this medication in elderly people, such as visual problems, confusion, even psychotic behavior and loss of temperature regulation. Avoid touching your eye after handling this patch and before washing your fingers, as this may result in dilation of the pupil and blurring of vision. This is generally not serious and will pass within 48 hours. Persons should avoid this product if they have glaucoma, are pregnant or are nursing, have liver or kidney disease, have a metabolic disorder, have trouble urinating, have obstructions of the stomach or intestine, or have very sensitive skin.

An excellent prescription drug that effectively treats nausea and vomiting from all causes, and which works very well in treating motion sickness, is Atarax. This medication is listed in the recommended prescription medical kit. Dosage for motion sickness treatment is one 25 mg tablet every four hours as needed.

Chapter 4

Sprains, Fractures, and Dislocations

ACUTE JOINT INJURY

Proper care of joint injuries must be started immediately. *R*est, *I*ce, *C*ompression, and *E*levation (RICE) form the basis of good first aid management. Cold should be applied for the first 2 days, as continuously as possible. Afterward, applying heat for 20 minutes, 4 times daily is helpful. Cold decreases the circulation, which lessens bleeding and swelling. Heat increases the circulation, which then aids the healing process. This method applies to all injuries including muscle contusions and bruises.

Elevate the involved joint, if possible. Wrap with an elastic bandage to immobilize the joint and provide moderate support once walking or use of the joint begins. Take care that the wrappings are not so tightly applied that they cut off the circulation.

Use crutches or other support to take enough weight off an injured ankle and knee to the point that increased pain is not experienced. The patient should not use an injured joint if use causes pain, as this indicates further strain on the already stressed ligaments or the existence of a fracture. Conversely, if use of the injured part does not cause pain, additional damage is not being done even if there is considerable swelling.

If the victim must walk on an injured ankle or knee, and doing so causes pain, then support it the best way possible (wrapping, crutches, decreased carrying load, tight boot for ankle injury) and realize that further damage is being done, but that in your opinion the situation warrants such a sacrifice.

Figure 6 A,B
Example of properly wrapped support dressing of figure eight technique around a knee and ankle.

Wrapping an ankle with an ace bandage is easy. The so-called figure eight technique is illustrated in figure 6A. Simply wrap around the ankle, under and around the foot and layer as shown.

Wrapping a knee is similarly performed using a figure eight technique, as shown in figure 6B. These wraps provide compression and slight support. They should never be applied so tight that they cause discomfort or cut off circulation.

Pain medications may be given as needed, but elevation and decreased use will provide considerable pain relief.

Dislocations

If the joint in question is deformed and/or the patient cannot move it, then the joint has suffered either a severe sprain or dislocation. Support the joint with sling or splinting in such a manner that further stress is not applied to the joint.

For the advanced treatment of specific dislocations, please refer to my book *Wilderness Medicine*. These techniques are beyond the scope of first aid, but if you are unable to obtain medical help, reductions of shoulder, elbow, finger, and nose dislocations can reduce pain and facilitate long evacuations.

Fractures

Fracture is the medical term for a broken bone. Fractures have several critical aspects to consider during management: 1) loss of circulation or nerve damage if bone spicules press against these structures due to deformity of the fracture; 2) introduction of infection if the skin is broken at or near the fracture site; 3) failure of the bone to mend properly due to improper alignment of bone fragments.

At times it will be uncertain whether or not a fracture actually exists. There will be point tenderness, frequently swelling and discoloration over the fracture site or the generalized area, and in obvious cases, deformity and loss of stability. If doubt exists, splint and treat for pain, avoiding the use of the involved part. Within a few days the pain will have diminished and the crises may be over. If not, the suspicion of fracture will loom even larger.

People frequently will say: "Well, I can move it, it must not be broken!" This is not true. The pain associated with activity may discourage movement, but it certainly does not prevent it. With proper splinting the pain involved with a fracture will decrease dramatically. Pain medication should be provided as soon as possible. A proper splint is well padded to protect underlying skin from developing pressure sores. It should also immobilize the joint above and below the fracture site. Fracture splinting requires common sense—and sometime imagination when fabricating some first aid device from available items such as ski poles, rolled newspapers, tree branches—even boots, eye glass frames, and articles of clothing.

Reduction, or correction, of fractures should be left to the hands of skilled persons. The adage "splint them as they lie" is the golden rule in handling fractures. However, if obvious circulation damage is occurring, namely the pulses beyond the fracture site have ceased, the extremity is turning blue and cold to the touch, or numbness is apparent in the portion of the limb beyond the fracture, angulations of the fracture should be straightened to attempt to eliminate the pressure damage. Broken bone edges can be very sharp—in fact a laceration of the blood vessels and nerves may have already occurred, thus causing the above symptoms.

Chapter 5

Bites and Stings

ANIMAL BITES

Animal bite wounds must be vigorously cleaned. While surgical scrubs (such as the Hibiclens recommended for your travel medical kit) are ideal, any *very* dilute solution of clean water and soap or detergent will work quite well. The wound should generally be covered with triple antibiotic ointment and a pressure dressing. The patient should be seen by a physician as soon as possible. Tetanus immunization must be current within 5 years.

Rabies

This disease can be transmitted on the North American continent by several species of mammals, namely skunk, bat, fox, coyote, racoon, bobcat, and wolf. Any unprovoked attack by one of these mammals should be considered an attack by a rabid animal. Dogs and cats in the United States have a low incidence of rabies. Information from local departments of health will indicate if rabies is currently of concern in these animals. *In many foreign countries the bite of a cat or dog should be considered rabid.* Animals whose bites have never caused rabies in humans in the US are livestock (cattle, sheep, horse), rabbit, gerbil, chipmunk, squirrel, rat, and mouse. Hawaii is the only rabies free state. Countries free of rabies are England, Australia, Japan, and parts of the Caribbean. In Europe the red fox is the animal most often rabid with documented cases spreading to dogs, cats, cattle, and deer. Canada's rabies occurs mostly in foxes and skunks in the province of Ontario. Mongoose rabies is found in South Africa and the Caribbean islands of Cuba, Puerto Rico, Hispaniola, and Grenada. In the United States there have been 11 cases of rabies reported between 1980 and 1989. In India 40,000 to 50,000 people die yearly from rabies, with an equal incidence in the other developing counties of Asia, Africa, and Latin America.

The treatment for rabies is initiated with Rabies Immune Globulin 20 IU/kg. Half is infiltrated around the wound and the remaining half is given IM in the gluteal area (upper outer quadrant of the bottom). Also, human diploid cell vaccine (HDCV) 1 ml must be given IM in the shoulder on days 0, 3, 7, 14, and 28.

Treatment of Insect Bites and Stings

Prevention of insect bites and stings is important for comfort and to minimize the chance of catching insect borne diseases. The use of insect repellent, sprays, netting, proper clothing, and avoiding the times and locations of significant insect swarming are all necessary techniques. This topic is discussed in Chapter 5.4 of the *Travelers' Medical Resource*.

Honey bee—also wasp, yellow jackets, and hornets are members of the order *Hymenoptera*. Stings from these insects hurt instantly and the pain lingers. The danger comes from the fact that some persons are "hypersensitive" to the venom and can have an immediate *anaphylactic shock* which is life-threatening. Fire ants and other insects may also cause an anaphylactic reaction.

The pain of stings and local skin reactions to bites can be alleviated by almost anything applied topically. Best choices are cold packs, dibucaine ointment from the medical kit, or a piece of Spenco 2nd Skin and the use of oral pain medication. Swelling can be prevented and/or treated with oral antihistamine such as Benadryl 25 mg taken 4 times daily.

The puss caterpillar (*Megalopyge opercularis*) of the southern US and the gypsy moth caterpillar (*Lymantria dispar*) of the northeastern US have bristles that cause an almost immediate skin rash and welt formation. Treatment includes patting the victim with a piece of adhesive tape to remove these bristles. Thoroughly cleanse the area with soap and water. A patch of Spenco 2nd Skin is very cooling. Give Benadryl 25 mg, one capsule 4 times daily.

Tick bites are of increased concern due to the diseases that can be transmitted by these little fellows. Lyme disease, Rocky Mountain spotted fever, Colorado tick fever, relapsing fever, tularemia, babesiosis, ehrlichiosis and tick paralysis are amongst the tick borne diseases found just in the United States. Remove the tick by grasping the victim's skin with the splinter forceps (tweezers) just where the tick has bitten the victim as illustrated in figure 1. Remove by pulling straight up, probably also taking a small piece of skin as the tick pincers hang on tightly. I have seldom found heating the tick with a hot paper clip, using alcohol, finger nail polish remover, or other chemical means very successful.

Anaphylactic Shock

While most commonly due to insect stings, this severe form of life-threatening shock may be encountered as a serious allergic reaction to medications, shell fish and other foods, or anything to which one has become profoundly allergic. Those developing anaphylaxis generally have warnings of their severe sensitivity in the form of welts (urticaria) forming all over their body immediately after exposure, the development of an asthmatic attack with respiratory wheezing, or the onset of symptoms of shock. After an exposure with such severe warning symptoms, the concern is that the next exposure might produce increased symptoms or even the shock state known as anaphylaxis.

This deadly form of shock can begin within seconds of exposure. It cannot be treated as shock would normally be handled, with elevation of the feet above heart level. The only life-saving remedy is to administer the drug called epinephrine (Adrenalin). It is available for emergency use as a component of a prepackaged prescription kit called the "Anakit" or in a special automatic injectable syringe called the EpiPen. Note illustrations of each type of kit in figure 7.

The Anakit is recommended as it contains two injections of epinephrine, rather than one and the cost is about half that of the EpiPen. Nor-

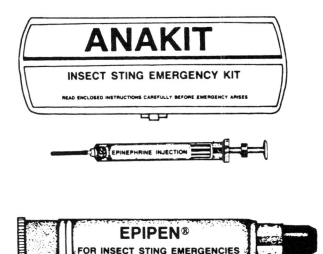

Figure 7
The "Anakit" and "EpiPen" used to treat severe insect reactions.

mal dosage is .3 cc for an adult of the 1:1000 epinephrine solution given "subQ" (in the fatty layer beneath the skin). This may have to be repeated in 15 to 20 minutes if the symptoms of wheezing or shock start to return. The Anakit contains a chewable antihistamine which should also be taken immediately, but antihistamines are of no value in treating the shock or asthmatic component of anaphylaxis.

Anyone experiencing anaphylactic reactions should be evacuated to medical care, even though they have responded to the epinephrine. They are at risk of the condition returning and they should be monitored carefully over the next 24 hours.

First Aid Management of Snake Bite

Snake bite prevention is easier than treatment. Wear boots that cover the ankle and avoid placing your hands or reaching into areas where your view is obstructed in habitats of poisonous snakes. Avoid poisonous snakes when seen, rather than trying to kill them. These steps will prevent most snake bite incidents from occurring

Nonpoisonous Snake Bite

Get away from the snake. Cleanse the bitten area with surgical scrub—apply suction with the Extractor to promote evacuation of puncture debris. No constriction band should be used. Treat for shock. Manage the wound as a puncture wound. The victim should have had a tetanus shot within 5 years.

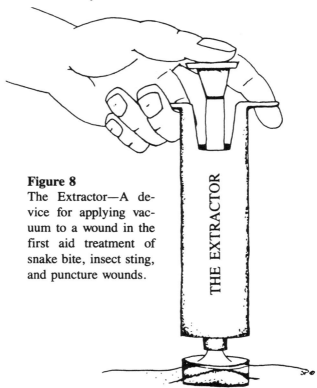

Figure 8
The Extractor—A device for applying vacuum to a wound in the first aid treatment of snake bite, insect sting, and puncture wounds.

Poisonous Snake Bite

Not everyone bitten by a poisonous snake will have envenomation injury—fully 20% of rattlesnake and 30% of cotton mouth water moccasin and copperhead bites will not envenomate during their bite. DO NOT APPLY COLD—this is associated with increased tissue damage. 1) Immobilize the injured part at heart level or slightly above in a position of function. 2) Apply an elastic bandage with a firm wrap from the bite site towards the body, leaving the bite exposed if you have an Extractor for further treatment, covered if you do not. 3) Apply suction with the Extractor (see figure 8). Making incisions actually decreases the amount of venom that can be removed with this device. If applied within 3 minutes as much as 35% of the venom may be removed with the Extractor. After $1/2$ hour, less than 3% more will be removed so further suction can be terminated. 4) Treat for shock and evacuate to professional medical help.

Antivenin and pharmacologic management of poisonous snake bites, to include cobra and other species, as well as specific therapies for poisonous spiders and scorpions, is discussed in *Wilderness Medicine.*

Chapter 6

Aquatic Injuries

CATFISH STINGS

Apply hot water as indicated under STING RAY. The wound must be properly cleaned and irrigated using surgical scrub, if available, or soap. Place the patient on an oral antibiotic for several days to decrease the chance of wound infection which is common with this injury. Treat an infected wound as described on page 6.

Coral Cuts, Barnacle Cuts

Clean the wound thoroughly—trivial wounds can later flare into real disasters that may go on for years. Scour thoroughly with a coarse cloth or soft brush and surgical scrub or soapy water. Then apply hydrogen peroxide to help bubble out fine particles and bacteria. Apply triple antibiotic ointment. Manage this wound as discussed in the section on laceration care.

Coral Stings
These injuries are treated as indicated under JELLYFISH.

Jellyfish
Tentacles can cause mild pricking to burning, shooting, terrible pain. The worse danger is shock and drowning. Avoid the use of hot water in treating this injury. First, pour ocean water over the injury. Try to remove the tentacles with gloved hands. Pour alcohol (or ideally formalin) over the wound, which will prevent the nematocysts from firing more poison. Both ammonia or vinegar would work, but not as well as formalin or alcohol. Urine may be used, but do not use fresh water. Powder the area with a dry powder such as flour or baking powder. Gently scrape off the mess with a knife, clam shell or other sharp instrument, but avoid cutting the nematocysts with a sharp blade. Apply hydrocortisone cream .5% four times daily from the Traveler's Medical Kit, or the prescription product Topicort .25% twice daily for inflammation.

Scorpion Fish
Same treatment as STING RAY.

Sea Urchin
Punctures from sea urchin spines cause severe pain and burning. Besides trauma from the sharp spines, some species inject a venom. The wound can appear red and swollen or even blue to black from a harmless dye which may be contained in the spines. Generalized symptoms are

rare, but may include weakness, numbness, muscle cramps, nausea, and occasionally shortness of breath. The spines should be removed thoroughly—a very tedious process. Very thin spines may be absorbed by the body without harm, but some may form a reactive tissue around them (granulomas) several months later. Spines may migrate into joints and cause pain and inhibit movement or lodge against a nerve and cause extreme pain. The discoloration of the dye causes no problems, but may be mistaken for a thin spine. Relief may be obtained by soaking in hot water (110° to 113° F) for 20 to 30 minutes. Vinegar or acetic acid soaks several times a day may help dissolve spines that are not found. Evacuation and treatment by a physician is advisable.

Sponge Rash

Sponges handled directly from the ocean can cause an allergic reaction that appears immediately. Fine spicules may also break off in the outer layer of skin also causing inflammation. It will be difficult to tell whether your victim is suffering from the allergic reaction or the spicules, or both. Soak the affected skin by applying vinegar to a cloth and covering for 15 minutes. Dry the skin and pat with the adhesive side of tape to remove sponge spicules. Again soak in vinegar for 5 minutes. An application of rubbing alcohol for 1 minute has been suggested. Then apply hydrocortisone cream .5% four times a day or Topicort .25% twice daily for several days until the inflammation subsides.

Sting Ray

The damage is done by the barbed tail, which lacerates the skin, imbedding pieces of tail material and venom into the wound. The wound bleeds heavily. Pain increases over 90 minutes and takes 6 to 48 hours to abate.

Immediately rinse the wound with sea water and remove any particles of the tail sheath which are visible as these particles continue to release venom. Hot water is the treatment of choice— applied as soon as possible and as hot as the patient can stand it (110°–113° F). The heat will destroy the toxin rapidly and remove the pain that the patient is experiencing. After hot water has been applied and all tail particles removed, the wound may be loosely closed with taping techniques. Elevation of the wound is important. If particularly dirty, leave the wound open and continue to use intermittent hot soaks 20 minutes at a time, every 2 hours. Questionably dirty wounds should be treated with Bactrim DS 1 tablet twice daily or doxycycline 100 mg twice daily. As these are nasty, painful wounds, treat for shock from the onset.

Chapter 7

Environmental Injuries

COLD WEATHER INJURIES

The term "hypothermia" refers to the lowering of the body's core temperature to 95° F (35° C); "profound hypothermia" is a core temperature lower than 90° F (32° C). Another important point is that the term "hypothermia" applies to two distinctly different diseases. One is "chronic hypothermia," the slow onset hypothermia of the outdoors traveler exposed to conditions too cold for their equipment to adequately protect them; the other is "acute," or "immersion hypothermia," the rapid onset hypothermia of a person immersed in cold water.

Hypothermia is the most likely of the environmental injuries that will be encountered in the outdoors. Prevention is the hall mark of survival, in fact hypothermia has been called the killer of the unprepared. It is most important to attempt to prevent hypothermia. The factors that protect trip members include being in good physical condition, maintaining adequate nutrition, prevention of physical exhaustion, prevention of dehydration, wearing adequate clothing, and having replacement clothing available in case of emergencies. More extensive information on various aspects of hypothermia prevention, diagnosis, and treatment can be found in my book *Hypothermia: Death by Exposure*, published by ICS Books.[2]

Chronic Hypothermia

The essential aspects of surviving this situation are: being prepared to prevent it, recognizing it when it occurs, and knowing how to treat it. Dampness and wind are the most devastating factors to be considered. Dampness as it can reduce the insulation of clothing and cause evaporative heat loss. Wind as the increased convection heat loss can readily strip away body energy, the so called "wind chill" effect. Remember, it is possible to die of hypothermia in temperatures far above freezing—in fact most hypothermia deaths occur in the 30° to 50° F (-1° to 10° C) range.

Detection of hypothermia is generally made by two observations. The first is to watch for exhaustion. Exhausted victims are not necessarily hypothermic, yet. But they will be unless they can obtain adequate rest and have adequate clothing to protect them from heat loss during rest, or after they actually reach exhaustion.

---

[2]*Hypothermia: Death by Exposure* is available from ICS Books, Inc., 107 East 89th Avenue, Merrillville, IN 46410, telephone (219) 769-0585 for $9.95 plus $1.50 handling.

"WIND CHILL CHART--FAHRENHEIT"

FAHRENHEIT WIND CHILL EQUIVALENT TEMPERATURE

Wind Speed MPH	TEMPERATURE FAHRENHEIT																					
	50	40	35	30	25	20	15	10	5	0	-5	-10	-15	-20	-25	-30	-35	-40	-45	-50	-55	-60
Calm	50	40	35	30	25	20	15	10	5	0	-5	-10	-15	-20	-25	-30	-35	-40	-45	-50	-55	-60
5	48	37	33	27	21	16	12	6	1	-5	-11	-15	-20	-26	-31	-35	-41	-47	-52	-57	-65	-70
10	40	28	21	16	9	4	-2	-9	-15	-24	-27	-33	-38	-46	-52	-58	-64	-70	-75	-83	-90	-95
15	36	22	16	9	1	-5	-11	-18	-25	-32	-40	-45	-51	-58	-65	-72	-77	-85	-90	-99	-105	-110
20	32	18	12	4	-4	-10	-17	-25	-32	-39	-46	-53	-60	-67	-75	-82	-89	-96	-102	-110	-115	-120
25	30	16	7	0	-7	-15	-22	-29	-37	-44	-52	-59	-67	-74	-83	-88	-96	-104	-111	-118	-125	-135
30	28	13	5	-2	-11	-18	-26	-33	-41	-48	-56	-63	-70	-79	-87	-94	-101	-109	-115	-125	-130	-140
35	27	11	3	-4	-13	-20	-27	-35	-43	-51	-60	-67	-72	-82	-90	-98	-105	-113	-120	-129	-135	-146
40	26	10	1	-6	-15	-21	-29	-37	-45	-53	-62	-69	-76	-85	-94	-100	-107	-115	-125	-132	-140	-150

Exposed Flesh Can Freeze in 60 Seconds

Exposed Flesh Can Freeze in 30 Seconds

NOTE 1: The above chart has been based upon the Siple Equation and reflects Wind Chill Equivalent temperatures in Fahrenheit.

NOTE 2: At low wind speeds, relative humidity and radiant heat are more important than wind speed in determining equivalent temperate comfort.

NOTE 3: Most charts indicate that at wind speeds over 40 mph there is little additional wind chill effect. This is a reflection of an error in the basic equation at these higher wind speeds and is not correct. Heat loss IS magnified by these higher wind speeds, but the chart is an accurate indicator of equivalent temperature at speeds lower than 40 mph.

TABLE 3
By knowing the speed of the wind and the temperature this chart can be used to calculate wind chill temperatures. The lower margin shows the breaking point where skin freezes in 60 seconds or 30 seconds.

SIGNS AND SYMPTOMS OF HYPOTHERMIA

CORE TEMP.	SIGNS AND SYMPTOMS
99° to 97°F (37° to 36°C)	Normal temperature range, Shivering may begin
97° to 95°F (36° to 35°C)	Cold sensation, goose bumps, unable to perform complex tasks with hands, shivering can be mild to severe, skin numb
95° to 93°F (35° to 34°C)	Shivering intense, muscle incoordination becomes apparent, movements slow and labored, stumbling pace, mild confusion, may appear alert, unable to walk 30 ft. line properly — BEST FIELD TEST FOR EARLY HYPOTHERMIA
93° to 90°F (34° to 32°C)	Violent shivering persists, difficulty speaking, sluggish thinking, amnesia starts to appear and may be retrograde, gross muscle movements sluggish, unable to use hands, stumbles frequently, difficulty speaking, signs of depression
90° to 86°F 32° to 30°C)	Shivering stops in chronic hypothermia, exposed skin blue or puffy, muscle coordination very poor with inability to walk, confusion, incoherent, irrational behavior, BUT MAY BE ABLE TO MAINTAIN POSTURE AND THE APPEARANCE OF PSYCHOLOGICAL CONTACT
86° to 82°F (30° to 27.7°C)	Muscles severely rigid, semiconscious, stupor, loss of psychological contact, pulse and respirations slow, pupils can dilate
82° to 78°F (27 to 25.5°C)	Unconsciousness, heart beat and respiration erratic, pulse and heart beat may be inapparent, muscle tendon reflexes cease
78° to 75°F (25° to 24°C)	Pulmonary edema, failure of cardiac and respiratory centers, probable death, DEATH MAY OCCUR BEFORE THIS LEVEL
64°F (17.7°C)	Lowest recorded temperature of chronic hypothermia survivor, Chicago 1951
48.2°F (9°C)	Lowest recorded temperature of induced hypothermia in surgical patient with survival, 1958

TABLE 4
Prevention against hypothermia is possible when symptoms are recognizable. The symptoms relative to the temperature are given in this table.

The second is loss of coordination. People who cannot walk a straight 30 foot (9 meter) line are hypothermic. This same test was formerly used by the police to detect inebriation, which also causes loss of coordination. Both impair mental process. For that reason, when hypothermia is detected in travelers, their judgement must be suspect. More than not trusting their decisions, these people actually need help. They must be treated for hypothermia.

The treatment for hypothermia is basically:

1. Prevent further heat loss. Wet clothing must be removed and replaced with dry clothing. At the very least, it must be covered with a rain jacket and pants— and this in turn covered with more insulation.
2. Treat dehydration. Hypothermia causes vasoconstriction which in effect shrinks the fluid volume of the victim. This is only one reason for dehydration, but all hypothermic people are, indeed, very dehydrated. This volume needs replacement.
3. Treat the victim gently. Very cold people can suffer cardiac rhythm problems if they are jarred around. If they are being carried during an evacuation, avoid bumping them along the ground or dropping them from a stretcher.
4. Add heat. If victims can stand, and you can build a fire, do it! And have them stand comfortably near it. A roaring fire can replace a massive number of calories and practically speaking, if patients can stand on their own by the fire, they are not so profoundly hypothermic that you

would have to worry about rewarming shock.

5. Avoid rewarming shock. Persons who are unable to stand are so ill that if they were reheated too rapidly, they could be adversely affected. The dehydration of hypothermia causes a substantial decrease in their fluid volume. So much so that a sudden rewarming can result in shock, even death. Note: this is a concern of the chronic hypothermic, not the acute (immersion) hypothermic victim.

6. Be aware of after-drop. As victims were being reheated it was noted that their core temperature continued to drop before starting to rise. This is called "after-drop." It was originally thought to be a cause of death, but the significant reason for death in the chronic hypothermic is actually rewarming shock. All persons will have after-drop, which is related to the rate of cooling that was taking place before the rewarming process started. It amounts to an equilibration phenomenon. After-drop *is* a serious problem in the treatment of acute (immersion) hypothermia, but is probably not of much concern in the chronic hypothermic.

7. Avoid adding cold. Never rub the person with snow or allow further exposure to the cold. It is probably best to avoid undressing the victim while exposed to the environment—do this in a sleeping bag or other sheltered area if at all possible. Try to warm water before giving the patient, if possible.

8. Allow rest. These patients are at or near exhaustion. Rest is mandatory to replace

the high energy compounds that are required to shiver, work, and otherwise
generate heat. If resting victims are being adequately insulated from further
heat loss, there is no reason why they
cannot be allowed to sleep. It is thera-
peutic. Do not shake or slap a hypothermic individual (see item 3 above).

Deepening hypothermia will lead to a semi-
comatose state and worse. This victim needs to
be evacuated to help. Wrap to prevent further
heat loss and transport. Chemical heat packs,
warmed rocks or water bottles, etc., can be
added to the wrap to help offset further heat loss,
but care must be taken not to burn the victim. If
evacuation is not feasible, heat will have to be
added slowly to avoid re-warming shock. Huddling with two rescuers naked with the victim in
an adequate sleeping bag may be the only alterna-
tive.

Acute Hypothermia
Acute hypothermia is the term applied to hypothermia which occurs in less than 2 hours.
This generally means cold water immersion. If
the air temperature and the water temperature
add to less than 100° F (38° C), there is a risk of
acute hypothermia if a person falls into the water.
As a rule of thumb, a person who has been in
water of 50°F (10° C) or less for a period of 20
minutes or longer, is suffering from a severe
amount of heat loss. That individual's thermal
mass has been so reduced that they are in potentially serious condition. They should not be allowed to move around as this will increase the
blood flow to their very cold skin and facilitate a
profound circulatory induced after-drop; one that

is so great as to be potentially lethal. If this same person is simply wrapped as a litter case and not provided outside heat, there is a real danger of them cooling below a lethal level due to this profound amount of heat loss.

The ideal treatment is rapid re-warming of the acute hypothermic by placing them in hot water (110° F, or 43° C), forcing rapid replacement of heat. These people may have an almost normal core temperature initially, but one that is destined to drop dramatically as their body equilibrates the heat store from their core to their very cold mantle. A roaring fire can be a life saver. If not available, huddling two naked rescuers with the victim in a large sleeping bag may be the only answer—the same therapy that might have to be employed in the field treatment of chronic hypothermia under some conditions.

Frostbite

Frostbite is the freezing of tissue. Surface skin goes through several phases before this occurs. The freezing process requires predisposing risk factors to be present before the events leading to frostbite are initiated. Outside temperatures must be below freezing for frostbite to occur, in fact skin temperature must be cooled to between 22° to 24° F (-5.5° C to-4.4° C) before tissue will freeze. The underlying physical condition of the victim, length of cold contact, and type of cold contact (such as cold metal or fuel) are other important factors leading to frostbite.

Traditionally, several degrees of frostbite are recognized. Generally, deeply frostbitten flesh will not indent when pressed upon, while superficial injury will also be waxy colored and cold, but will indent. When superficial frost bite is suspected, thaw immediately so that it does not be-

come a more serious, deep frostbite. Warm the
hands by withdrawing them into the parka
through the sleeves—avoid opening the front of
the parka to minimize heat loss. Feet should be
thawed against a companion or cupped in your
own hands in a roomy sleeping bag, or otherwise
in an insulated environment. NEVER, NEVER
rub snow on a frostbitten area.

For victims with deep frostbite, rapid rewarming in 110° F (43° C) water is the most
effective treatment. This thawing may take 20 to
30 minutes, but it should be continued until all
paleness of the tips of the fingers or toes has
turned pink or burgundy red, but no longer. This
will be very painful and will require pain medication. Refreezing would result in substantial tissue
loss. The frozen part should not be thawed if
there is any possibility of refreezing the part.
Also, once the victim has been thawed, very
careful management of the thawed part is required. The patient will become a stretcher case
if the foot is involved. For that reason, it may be
necessary to leave the foot or leg(s) frozen and
allow the victim to walk back to the evacuation
point. Tissue damage increases with the length of
time that it is allowed to remain frozen, but this
damage is less than the refreezing destruction.

Immersion Foot

It is essential that anyone going into the outdoors know how to prevent this injury. It results
from wet, cool conditions with temperature expo-
sures from 68° F (20° C) down to freezing. To
prevent this problem avoid non-breathing (rubber) footwear when possible, dry the feet and
change wool or polypro socks when feet become
wet or sweaty (every 3 to 4 hours, at minimum),
and periodically elevate, air, dry, and massage

the feet to promote circulation. Avoid tight, constrictive clothing. *At night footwear must absolutely be removed and socks changed to dry ones, or simply removed and feet dried before retiring to the sleeping bag.*

There are two clinical stages of immersion foot. In the initial stage the foot is cold, swollen, waxy, mottled with dark burgundy to blue splotches. This foot is spongy to touch, whereas the frozen foot is very hard. Skin is sodden and friable. Loss of feeling makes walking difficult. The second stage lasts from days to weeks. The feet are swollen, red and hot. Blisters form and infection and gangrene are common problems. The pain from immersion foot can be life-long and massive tissue injury can easily develop.

Treatment would include providing the victim 10 grains of aspirin every 6 hours to help decrease platelet adhesion and promote blood circulation. This injury is one of the few medical situations in which alcohol plays a proper role. Providing 1 ounce of hard liquor every hour while awake and 2 ounces every 2 hours during sleeping hours, helps vasodilate and increase the flow of blood to the feet. Immediate stretcher evacuation is necessary.

Other cold injuries such as chilblains, frozen lung, etc., are less threatening and will not seriously injure trip participants. A full treatment of the prevention, diagnosis, and treatment of cold injuries is covered in my book *Hypothermia: Death by Exposure.*

SUN AND HEAT INJURIES
Ultraviolet radiation causing sun burns, eye injuries, and other skin damage, and infrared rays potentially leading to the various forms of illness caused by over-heating, result in many un-

comfortable and even lethal situations for the unwary traveler.

Sun and snow blindness is discussed in the section on eye injuries found on page 12 in this manual.

Prickly Heat

Prickly heat is a common problem many people have on exposure to hot, even sub-tropical sun. It is caused by the closure of sweat glands which leads to the formation of small, red blisters on mildly pink skin. This problem is encountered in areas of the body which tend to stay damp or which tend to have contact with damp clothing—such as under the arm pits, hollow of the knee, front of the elbows and forearm, over the collar-bone and the front of the chest.

Two factors cause this sogginess. One is high humidity which prevents sweat evaporation as the atmosphere is already saturated. The second is wearing clothes that either prevent sweat from evaporating or from being absorbed. Clothes that help sweat evaporate are loose-fitting. This provides an essential layer of air between the garment and the skin. Fabrics should be chosen that have a high moisture absorption capability, such as cotton, as these wick moisture away from the skin.

It has also been shown that providing adequate air conditioning for 8 hours a day tends to decrease the incidence of prickly heat. British army studies demonstrate a peak incidence of prickly heat after 4 to 5 months of exposure to high humidity-heat conditions, so the average tourist should be spared this malady.

Treatment is accomplished with thorough drying of the skin, bathing with a bland soap, application of drying powders, and seeking increased time in air-conditioned settings.

Sun Burn

Infrared rays from the sun provide heat, but do not burn or tan skin. Long-wave ultraviolet rays, called UVA, between 320 and 400 nanometers cause most drug-induced sun reactions, which can be a problem when the traveler is taking doxycycline or a sulfa drug (such as Bactrim), frequently used to prevent diarrhea or treat infection. Midrange ultraviolet light (UVB), between 290 and 320 nanometers, is the major cause of sunburn. In temperate latitudes only a small portion of UVB reaches the earth's surface before 10:00 AM, or after 3:00 PM. UVA reaches the ground fairly constantly throughout the daylight hours.

Most sun screens are designed to block UVB, but do not block UVA. For persons using the above drugs, special care must be taken during any daylight hours to minimize the chance of a drug reaction. Proper attire, consisting of large brimmed hats and tight knit, dry clothing that covers the front of the neck and the extremities, is a must. Many solar dermatitis reactions are seen in the "V" of the neck, arms, nape of the neck, and legs. Wet clothing, or loosely knit cloth, can allow UV radiation penetration and thus do not provide adequate protection.

People with a pale complexion are at the greatest risk from sun burn. While they need to be primarily concerned about UVB radiation, even a 60 minute exposure to UVA will result in a burn. As mentioned above, the morning and evening hours provide safe initial exposure times, except from UVA. It is best to limit sun exposure on non-tan body surfaces to a 15 minute exposure the first day, 30 minutes the next, 1 hour the day after and increasing exposure times by 1 hour daily from then on. Within 2 weeks, naked skin is tanned adequately to prevent sun burn with even an all day exposure. Problems of sun related skin aging and increased cancer risk remain a concern. Sunblocks are opaque preparations containing titanium dioxide, talc, or zinc oxide that scatter light, preventing any solar ultraviolet radiation from reaching the skin surface. Originally white, there are fashionable brands now available in various bright colors. These products are useful on limited areas, such as the nose, lips and tips of ears.

Sun Protection Factor is a term applied to sun screens that describes the *additional* time that a person may be exposed to the same intensity of sunlight and have the same amount of skin erythema, or reaction. If a person who would normally burn in 1 hour of exposure were to wear a sunscreen with a SPF rating of 5, that person could tolerate 5 hours of sun exposure to reach the same level of burn. Sunscreens are commonly sold with SPF ratings of 2 to 15. Some newly developed products are now available with SPF ratings of 50, allowing a theoretical exposure time beyond the hours of sunlight availability.

The SPF ratings given by the manufacturer can be misleading for several reasons. In 1982 a study of 30 sunscreen products labeled SPF 15 found that none had an actual SPF of greater than 12! Proper application is also very important. Applying too thin of a coat decreases the SPF automatically. The official amount that should be applied is 2 mg/cm::, but your guess is as good as mine as to how thick that turns out to be. Sunscreens are most effective when applied 30 minutes to 1 hour before sun exposure. This allows adequate penetration of the skin. They must be reapplied after sweating or swimming. Waterproof and water-resistant products will still be removed by sweating or toweling off and must be reapplied.

Multiple applications, however, do not increase the SPF rating of the product. For example, if a SPF 5 product is used, the amount of skin redness that develops in 5 hours will not be decreased by multiple applications of this product.

The SPF factor protection increases dramatically the higher the protection rating as indicated in the table below:

Table 5
Sun Protective Factor versus
Percentage of UV Protection

SPF	Percent Protection
2	50
4	75
8	87
15	93
29	97

Thus, sun protective factor ratings of 15 or greater should be chosen for adequate UV protection. Eighty percent of sun exposure is acquired during the first 20 years of life. The deadly skin cancer called melanoma is directly related to the amount of blistering sunburn received as a child. The incidence of this deadly condition has increased alarmingly. In 1933 the incidence was one case per 10,000 members of the U.S. population. In 1988 the frequency became one case per 150, and in 1990 the estimated frequency is one case per 100 members of our population!

Most sun screen formula do not protect the traveler from ultraviolet A damage. The only products that provide some protection from UVA are those containing benzophenones and anthranilates, other than the sun blocks mentioned above.

An increase in elevation places a person at more risk from ultraviolet exposure. Each 1,000 foot gain in elevation increases the intensity of the UV effect by 4%. These means that the intensity of sunlight at 5000 feet is greater than that experienced at sea level by 20%.

As mentioned under snow blindness, reflection from snow, sand, and water can increase the effect of this radiation by up to 100%! Not only is this reflective light additive, but the UV radiation can also strike areas of skin that are not normally exposed and are therefore more vulnerable to burn.

Wet skin may make the bather feel cooler, but it does nothing to protect from UV damage or sun burn. UV light can significantly penetrate one fourth an inch of water. Bright cloudy days will block the infrared heat rays from the sun, but will allow 60 to 80% of the ultraviolet rays through.

Many a vacation has been ruined in the attempt to soak up too much sun by beach and pool. One indiscreet hour too many and the traveler will not only be in excruciating pain, but will be readily avoiding all contact with the sun for the next two weeks!

In case of a sun burn, one of the best products to apply would be sheets of Spenco 2nd Skin. This is sold at most athletic supply stores and at many pharmacies across the US. It provides immediate pain relief and helps the skin heal rapidly. Various "caine" ointments and creams are sold for anesthetizing burnt skin. Creams and foams sold to treat hemorrhoids actually make good sun burn creams. Traditional burn ointments provide less relief, but aid in treating this problem. Cold compresses are useful for significant, immediate relief, but most burn victims easily become quite cold and care must be taken not to cool them too much. Oral pain medications are frequently required.

Heat Cramps

Salt depletion can result in nausea, twitching of muscle groups and at times severe cramping of abdominal muscles, legs, or elsewhere. Treatment consists of stretching the muscles involved (avoid overly aggressive massage), resting in a cool environment, and replacing salt losses. Generally 10 to 15 grams ($^1/_3$ to $^1/_2$ oz) of salt and generous water replacement should be adequate treatment.

Heat Exhaustion

This is a classic example of SHOCK, but in this case encountered while working in a hot environment and due to a heat stress injury. The body has dilated the blood vessels in the skin, attempting to divert heat from the core to the surface for cooling. However, this dilation is so pronounced, coupled with the profuse sweating and loss of fluid—also a part of the cooling process— that the blood pressure to the entire system falls too low to adequately supply the brain and the other organs. The patient will have a rapid heart rate, and will have the other findings associated with shock: Pale color, nausea, dizziness, headache, and a light-headed feeling. Generally the patient is sweating profusely, but this may not be the case. Skin temperature may be low, normal, or mildly elevated.

Treat for shock. Have the patient lie down immediately, and elevate the feet to increase the blood supply to the head. Also, provide copious water; 10 to 15 grams of salt would also be helpful, but water is the most important. Give a minimum of 1 to 2 quarts. Obviously, fluids can only be administered if the patient is conscious. If unconscious, elevate the feet 3 feet above head level and try to protect from the potential of accidentally inhaling vomit. Try to revive with stimulation, such as contact with the person or, if available, an ammonia inhalant. Give water when the patient awakens.

Heat Stroke

Heat stroke, or sun stroke as it is also called, represents the complete breakdown of the heat control process (thermal regulation). There is a total loss of the ability to sweat, core temperatures rise over 105° F (40.5° C) *rapidly* and will soon exceed 115° F (46° C) and result in death if this condition is not treated aggressively. THIS IS A TRUE MEDICAL EMERGENCY. The patient will be confused and rapidly become unconscious.

Immediately move the victim into shade or erect a hasty barrier for shade. If possible employ immediate immersion in ice water to lower the temperature. Once the core temperature lowers to 102° F the victim is removed and the temperature carefully monitored. It may continue to fall or suddenly rise again.

Further cooling with wet cloths may suffice. IV solutions of normal saline are started in the clinic setting—otherwise, douse the victim with the coolest water possible. Massage limbs to allow the cooler blood of the extremities to return to the core circulation more readily. Sacrifice your water or other beverage supply if necessary, fan and massage to provide the best coolant effect possible. Heat stroke victims should be evacuated as soon as possible, for their thermal regulation mechanism is quite unstable and will be labile for an unknown length of time. They should be placed under a physician's care as soon as possible.

HIGH ALTITUDE ILLNESS

The high altitude related illnesses can generally be avoided by gradual exposure to higher elevation, with the ascent rate not exceeding 1,000 feet per day when above 6,000 feet. The three major clinical manifestations of this disease complex are outlined below:

Acute Mountain Sickness (AMS)

Rarely encountered below 6,500 feet (2,000 meters), it is common in persons going above 10,000 feet (3,000 meters) without taking the time to acclimatize for altitude. Symptoms beginning soon after ascent consist of headache (often severe), nausea, vomiting, shortness of breath, weakness, sleep disturbance and occasionally a periodic breathing known to physicians as Cheyne-Stokes breathing.

Prevention, as with all of the high altitude illness problems, is gradual ascent to any altitude above 9,000 feet and light physical activity for the first several days. For persons especially prone to AMS, it may be helpful to take acetazolamide (Diamox) 250 mg every 12 hours starting the day before ascent and continuing the next 3 to 5 days. This prescription drug should be added to your medical kit if you expect rapid ascents of elevations above 9,000 feet.

Treatment is descent and relief can often be felt even if the descent is only 2,000 to 3,000 feet (600 to 900 meters). Full relief can be obtained by descending to below 6,500 feet (2,000 meters). Stricken individuals should avoid heavy exercise, but sleep does not help as the breathing is slower during sleep and oxygen deprivation is worse. Oxygen will only help if taken continuously for 12 to 48 hours. Aspirin may be used for headache. Mobigesic from the non-prescription kit may be used. In addition to descent, Decadron (dexamethasone) 4 mg tablets every 6 hours until below the altitude at which symptoms appeared has been shown to help treat AMS. Decadron tablets should be added to your medical kit if you expect to encounter elevations above 9,000 feet.

High Altitude Pulmonary Edema (HAPE)

This problem is rare below 8,000 feet (2,50 meters), but occurs at higher altitude in those poorly acclimatized. It is more prone to occur in persons between the ages of 5 and 18 (the incidence is apparently less than .4% in persons over 21 and as high as 6% in those younger); in persons who have had this problem before; and in persons who have been altitude acclimatized and who are returning to high altitude after spending 2 or more weeks at sea level.

Symptoms develop slowly within 24 to 60 hours of arrival at high altitude with shortness of breath, irritating cough, weakness, rapid heart rate and headache which rapidly progress to intractable cough with bloody sputum, low-grade fever and increasing chest congestion. Symptoms may progress at night. Climbers should be evaluated by listening to their chests for a fine crackling sound (called rales) and have their resting pulse rate checked nightly. A pulse rate of greater than 110 per minute or respirations greater than 16 per minute after a 20 minute rest is an early sign of HAPE. Respirations over 20 per minute and pulse over 120 per minute indicates a medical emergency and the patient must be evacuated immediately. Without treatment, death usually occurs within 6 to 12 hours after onset of coma.

Descent to lower altitude is essential and should not be delayed. Oxygen may be of value if given continuously over the next 12 to 48 hours, starting at 6 liters/minute for the first 15 minutes, then reduced to 2 liters/minute. A snug face mask is better than nasal prongs. Oxygen may provide rapid relief in mild cases, however it should be continued for a minimum of 6 to 12 hours, if possible. Oxygen is not a substitute for descent in severe cases. A descent of as little as 2,000 to 3,000 feet (600 to 900 meters) may result in prompt improvement. Further methods of treatment are described in *Wilderness Medicine*.

Cerebral Edema (CE)

This is a less common event than AMS or HAPE just mentioned, but it is more dangerous. Death has occurred from CE at altitude as low as 8,000 feet (2,500 meters), but CE is rare below 11,500 feet (3,500 meters). The symptoms are increasingly severe headache, mental confusion, emotional behavior, hallucinations, unstable gait, loss of vision, loss of dexterity, and facial muscle paralysis. The victim may fall into a restless sleep, followed by a deep coma and death.

Descent is essential. Oxygen should be administered. Decadron (dexamethasone) should be given in large doses, namely 10 mg intravenous, followed by 4 mg every 6 hours intramuscular until the symptoms subside. Response is usually noted within 12 to 24 hours and the dosage may be reduced after 2 to 4 days and gradually discontinued over a period of 5 to 7 days. Immediate descent and oxygen are recommended to prevent permanent neurological damage or death.

As can be noted from the above discussions of AMS, HAPE, and CE, the symptoms progress rather insidiously. They are not clear-cut, separate diseases—they often occur together. The essential therapy for each of them is recognition and descent. This is life saving and more valuable than the administration of oxygen or the drugs mentioned. To prevent them it is helpful to "climb high, but camp low"—ie, spend nights at the lowest camp elevation feasible.

Chapter 8

Travelers'
Medical Kit

This select list of medications and equipment relies primarily on non-prescription products to reduce the cost and the problems of acquiring safe and effective components. A list of suggested prescription items is included and described that is keyed to the *Travelers' Self Care Manual* and to the main text of the *Travelers' Medical Resource*. An additional section is included for adding special use drugs for certain travel conditions (such as malaria prophylaxis, acute mountain sickness prophylaxis, etc), as well as personal prescription medications. Finally, a location for telephone numbers, addresses, and other information that might be required in a medical emergency is included.

NON-PRESCRIPTION KIT COMPONENTS

Item: *Spenco 2nd Skin Blister Kit*

Qty: 1 kit

Purpose: Blister and burn treatment

This kit is truly a major advance in first aid. This inert hydrogel consists of 96% water and 4% polyethylene oxide. It is used on wet, weeping wounds to absorb these fluids and to protect the injury. This is a perfect prevention and even cure for friction blisters. It revolutionized the field treatment of 1st, 2nd, and 3rd degree burns, as it can be applied to all three as a perfect sterile covering and for pain relief. This item should be in every medical kit. The ideal covering pad is the Spenco Adhesive Knit Bandage, which comes with the Blister Kit. If used in treating hot spots, remove only the outer covering of cellophane from the Second Skin, cover with the Knit Bandaging, and occasionally dampen with clean water to maintain the hydrogel's hydration. For treatment of developed blisters, apply as above, but remove the top layer of cellophane also before applying the knit bandaging. Moisten as above. This product should not be confused with "Nu Skin" which is useless for treatment of the above problems

Item: *Potable Aqua and 1 liter poly bottle*

Qty: 1 bottle of 50 tablets/1 poly bottle

Purpose: Water purification and storage

Add one tablet per quart of water and allow to stand for 10 minutes prior to consumption. If the water is cloudy, let stand 20 minutes; if very cold increase the waiting period to 30 minutes.

Item: *Hibiclens Surgical Scrub*

Qty: 4 ounces

Purpose: Cleanse and disinfect wounds

This Stuart Pharmaceutical Company product [chlorhexidine gluconate 4%] far surpasses hexachlorophene (pHiso-Hex) and povidone-iodine (Betadine) scrub in its antiseptic action. Its onset and duration of action is also much more impressive than either of those two products. It is safe to use on skin and in open wounds. It should be irrigated from the eye, but will not cause damage with a short period of contact.

Item: *Cover-Strip*

Qty: 1 pkg of 6 each $1/2''$ × $4''$ strips

Purpose: Wound closure tapes

Several brands are available such as Cover-Strip by Beiersdorf, Steri-Strip by 3-M Corp, or even Butterfly Closures by Johnson & Johnson. Cover-Strips are perhaps the best tape wound closure system that can be obtained. These strips can be removed and re-applied while trying to adjust the wound edges and yet they will still retain their adhesive property, a quality that other products do not do as well. These strips breathe and can be left on as long as necessary for the wound to heal, often without an outer covering. Far better than "butterfly" bandages, the latter can be substituted if cost and availability is a factor.

Item: *Triple Antibiotic Ointment*

Qty: 1 one ounce tube

Purpose: Surface wound antibiotic protection

Each gram of this ointment contains bacitracin 400 units, neomycin sulfate 5 mg and polymyxin B sulfate 5000 units. For use as a topical antibiotic in the prevention and treatment of minor infections of abrasions and burns. A light coat should be applied twice daily. If a rash develops after use, it may mean a sensitivity to this product and its use should be discontinued.

Item: *Splinter Forceps*

Qty: 1 pair

Purpose: Splinter removal

Splinter forceps are fine pointed tweezers used to remove foreign bodies from the skin. Regular tweezers may be substituted.

Item: *#11 Scalpel Blade*

Qty: 1

Purpose: Sharp knife blade

This sharp instrument is used to uncover splinters, open boils or blisters, and for other minor procedures. A sharp knife blade can substitute, but it would not be as thin or as sharp.

Item: *Q-Tips*

Qty: 10 pkgs of 2 each, sterile

Purpose: Sterile applicator

Q-Tips can be used to remove foreign bodies from the eye, cleanse wounds, apply medications, or even used as a tooth pick.

Item: *Tape, ¹/₂ Inch*

Qty : 1 Roll

Purpose: Splinting, taping bandages

Old fashion water-proof tape is more versatile than newer knit tapes.

Item: *Actifed*

Qty: 24 Tablets

Purpose: Decongestant

Each tablet contains 60 mg of pseudoephedrine (a vasoconstrictor that dries up mucous formation) and 2.5 mg of triprolidine (an antihistamine to block allergic reactions). Normal dose is 1 tablet every 6 hours to relieve congestion in nasal and sinus passages, and to treat pressure in the middle ear due to eustachian tube blockage.

Item: *Bulb Syringe*

Qty: 1

Purpose: Wound irrigation

A bulb syringe easily and safely jets water into a wound with considerable force to remove residue that would allow infection. It can also be used to remove foreign bodies due to rinsing action as described in the text.

Item: *Antacid Tablets*

Qty: 24 tablets

Purpose: Treat stomach acid

Be sure to choose high potency antacid tablets. Various brands may be substituted, but do not forget an antacid!

Item: *Meclizine 25 mg*

Qty: 10 tablets

Purpose: Treat nausea, motion sickness

This item is very effective for nausea and vomiting, particularly when due to motion sickness. Dosage is 1 tablet daily. While sold non-Rx only for motion sickness, with prescription this may be taken 3 times daily for dizziness due to inner ear dysfunction. It will work against nausea from virtually any cause.

Item: *Benadryl 25 mg*

Generic Name: Diphenhydramine

Qty: 24 capsules

Purpose: Antihistamine

These capsules can be taken 1 or 2 every 6 hours to suppress allergy conditions of the skin and allergy or viral induced congestion. Benadryl is also a powerful cough suppressor, the dose being 1 capsule every 6 hours.

Item: *Mobigesic* (or equal)

Qty: 24 tablets

Purpose: Pain relief

A powerful, yet non-prescription, medication, Mobigesic relieves pain, fever, inflammation, and muscle spasm. Each tablet contains 325 mg of magnesium salicylate and 30 mg of phenyltoloxamine citrate. Ideal for arthritis and injuries of joints and muscles, as well as aches from infections. One of the most useful non-Rx drugs obtainable.

Item: *Hydrocortisone Cream .5%*

Qty: 1 ounce

Purpose: Skin allergy

This non-Rx steroid cream treats allergic skin rashes, such as those from poison ivy. A cream is ideal for treating weeping lesions, as opposed to dry scaly ones, but will work on either. To potentiate this medication apply an occlusive dressing (plastic cover) overnight.

Item: *Miconazole Cream 2%*

Qty: 1 ounce

Purpose: Antifungal

This is one of the most effective antifungal preparations available for foot, groin, or body fungal infections. Brand names are Monistat Derm and Micatin. The former is sold by Rx only, but Micatin and the generic product have been available without Rx since 1983.

Item: *Diasorb*

Qty: 24 Tablets

Purpose: Anti-diarrhea

The safest non-Rx anti-diarrhea agent made, it works as well as Imodium, which is a strong antimotility product. Available in liquid or tablets, the latter are easier to carry. Take 4 tablets at the first sign of diarrhea and repeat after each subsequent bowel movement or every 2 hours, whichever comes first. Maximum dose for an adult is 12 tablets per day. Use 2 tablets for children 6–12 and 1 tablet for children 3–6. Tablets should not be chewed, but rather swallowed whole with water. Carry the liquid for children who cannot swallow pills. This product controls diarrhea, but it also does not trap dangerous bacteria or parasites in the bowel as the indiscriminate use of Imodium or Lomotil is apt to due.

Item: *Imodium 2 mg*

Generic Name: Loperamide

Qty: 12 capsules

Purpose: Diarrhea

Imodium brand of loperamide lessens the secretion of fluid into the colon and decreases excess cramping of the colon, thus stopping diarrhea. It must be used with caution, especially if bloody diarrhea is present. A bloody diarrhea can indicate invasive organisms which will cause more harm if trapped in the colon. It is very effective, however, and provides rapid, symptomatic relief of diarrhea. The dose is two capsules immediately, followed by one capsule after each loose stool, up to a maximum of eight capsules per day. A pediatric form of liquid Imodium is also available without a prescription. Note the further description concerning the treatment of diarrhea on page 26.

PRESCRIPTION MEDICATIONS
The following prescription items may be necessary for use in prevention or treatment of medical problems during your travels. The quantities suggested are meant to support one person for treatment, not prophylaxis, purposes. Two antibiotics have been suggested for this kit. One or the other should suffice. These have been chosen based on their wide spectrum of activity against common travel infections, their general low level of side effects, and their reasonable cost. Your physician may suggest an alternate antibiotic. This information can then be entered into the notebook section of this handbook.

Suggested Prescription Kit Components

Item: *Doxycycline 100 mg*

Qty: 10

Purpose: Antibiotic

This antibiotic can be used to treat diarrhea and most infections at a dose of one tablet taken twice daily. When used for prevention of traveler's diarrhea or malaria prophylaxis the dosage is one tablet taken once daily. This product is not to be used in children 8 years or younger or during pregnancy. It may cause skin sensitivity on exposure to sunlight, thus causing an exaggerated sunburn. This does not usually happen, but be cautious during your first sun exposure when on this product. Many people traveling in the tropics have used this antibiotic safely. Common brand names are Vibramycin, Vibra-tabs, Vivox, and Doryx. Recommended quantity of 10 tablets would have to be increased if this medication is being used for disease prophylaxis rather than treatment.

Item: *Bactrim DS*

Generic Name: Sulfamethoxazole/
trimethoprim

Qty: 10 tablets

Purpose: Antibiotic

This is a brand name of a combination of two antibiotics, namely 800 mg of sulfamethoxazole and 160 mg of trimethoprim. Another common brand name is Septra DS. It is useful in treating traveler's diarrhea and many other infections utilizing a dose of one tablet twice daily. It should not be used at term of pregnancy or when nursing. Stop using in case of a skin rash as this may precede a more serious reaction. When used to prevent traveler's diarrhea, the dose is one tablet taken once daily. This product can also cause photosensitization, as indicated under doxycycline listed above.

Item: *Tobrex Ophthalmic Ointment .3%*

Generic Name: Tobramycin

Qty: $^{1}/_{8}$ ounce tube

Purpose: Antibiotic ointment for eye and
ear

Tobrex is a brand name for tobramycin ophthalmic ointment. While designed as an antibiotic for the eye, it is safe to apply to infected ear canals. This is useable on any surface infection, but too expensive to be carried for general skin use.

Item: *Pontocaine Ophthalmic Ointment .5%*

Generic Name: Tetracaine

Qty: $1/8$ ounce tube

Purpose: Eye pain

This sterile medication is packed especially for use in the eye, but it can be used to numb pain on the eye surface or to treat ear pain. Do not reapply to eye if pain returns without examining for the presence of a foreign body on the eye surface very carefully. Apply once daily as needed for eye pain. Do not use in an ear if there is considerable drainage as an ear drum may have ruptured—avoid use if ear drum is ruptured. Allow to melt into the ear canal and do not poke it in with a Q-Tip.

Item: *Topicort ointment .25%*

Generic Name: Desoximetasone

Qty: $1/2$ ounce tube

Purpose: Allergic skin reactions

This prescription steroid ointment treats severe allergic skin rashes. Ointments work best on dry, scaly lesions. Weeping, blistered areas are best treated with creams, or even wet soaks of dilute salt solution. Dosage is a thin coat twice daily. It should be used with caution over large body surface areas or in children. Use should be limited to 10 days or less.

Item: *Carafate 1 gram*

Generic Name: Sucralfate

Qty: 20 or more

Purpose: Heartburn or ulcer

Carafate is the brand name of sucralfate, an aluminum starch complex that heals and prevents ulcers and other damage to the gastric system from acid, medications, or other irritants. It does not affect acidity in the stomach, which is a plus for travelers. Reduced stomach acidity makes a person more vulnerable to bacteria and virus infections potentially causing traveler's diarrhea. Its healing action is due to a coating process. Very little is absorbed into the blood stream. This is a safe medication with few side effects.

Item *Atarax 25 mg tablet*

Generic Name: Hydroxyzine

Qty: 20 tablets

Purpose: nausea, anti-histamine, pain medication augmentation

Atarax is the brand name of hydroxyzine hydrochloride. These tablets have multiple uses. They are a very powerful anti-nausea agent, muscle relaxer, antihistamine, anti-anxiety agent, sleeping pill, and narcotic potentiator. For sleep 50 mg at bed time; for nausea 25 mg every 4 to 6 hours; to potentiate a narcotic, take two 25 mg tablets with each dose of the pain medication.

This medication helps with rashes of all types and has a drying effect on congestion.

Item *Tylenol #3*

Generic Name: Acetaminophen/codeine

Qty: 24 tablets

Purpose: pain, diarrhea, cough

Tylenol #3 is the brand name of a combination of 300 mg of acetaminophen and 30 mg of codeine phosphate. The principle use of this drug is in the relief of pain. Codeine is one of the most powerful cough suppression and anti-diarrhea agents known. Also useful in treating abdominal cramping. The dosage of 1 tablet every 4 hours will normally control a toothache. Maximum dosage is 2 tablets every 3 to 4 hours, augmented with Atarax—see above. Codeine tablets can be obtained without the acetaminophen, but they are considered a Class II narcotic which increases the difficulty of obtaining a prescription and which could complicate border crossing inquiries. Tylenol #3 is considered a Class III narcotic, even though the codeine content per tablet is the same strength as in the more restricted plain codeine tablet.

Item: *Transderm Scōp*

Generic Name: Scopolamine

Qty: 1 box of 4 patches

Purpose: To prevent motion sickness

Transderm Scōp, a patch containing scopolamine, has been developed for prevention of motion sickness using the transdermal method of providing medication. Each patch may be worn behind the ear for 3 days. It is fairly expensive, but very worth while if you are prone to this malady. There tends to be a higher frequency of side effects with this medication in elderly people, such as visual problems, confusion, and loss of temperature regulation.

The point of application for the Transderm Scōp patch, used to prevent motion sickness.

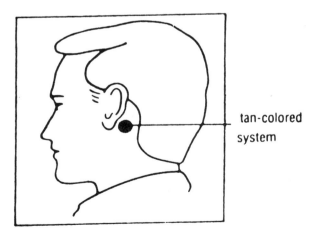

tan-colored
system

Augmenting Your Medical Kit

Additional quantities, substitutions for the above recommended products, and additional components may be indicated depending upon the traveler's activities, destination, remoteness from identified sources of acceptable medical help, and personal medical history. The best source for advice on these changes would be your physician or a travel medicine clinic in conjunction with your physician. The chapter on "Obtaining Help" in the *Travelers' Medical Resource* lists addresses and telephone numbers of many travel medical clinics and specialists who may be able to help you if you do not have a personal physician who is interested in travel medicine.

There are a variety of items that you will want to consider carrying on your trip. While some of these are not medical supplies, their existence can make your medical "survival" and comfort much more likely.

You cannot bring too many zip-lock baggies. They seem to have dozens of uses, and more keep presenting themselves all of the time.

Carry a strong 1 quart poly bottle in which to purify or carry water. It may be a long time between safe sources of water. Carry some water purification tablets, even if you do not think you may need to use them. While the non-prescription kit mentioned above includes Potable Aqua and a poly bottle for a water purification system, a coffee cup heating coil may suffice for many travelers. Be certain to also include a electrical current conversion system when traveling overseas, or the heating coil may not be operable.

Carry some high calorie trail munchies—edible food may be scarce at times for a number of reasons.

Keep medication in carry-on luggage to help

with compliance in following prescribed dosage times, prevent loss, and to serve as a rough medical history in an emergency.

Persons with chronic illnesses should wear a "Medic Alert" bracelet or other attention getting device listing their disabilities. The address for Medic Alert is : Medical Alert Foundation International, Turlock, CA 95381-1009. Telephone is 1-800-ID-ALERT (1-800-736-3342).

Consideration should be given to a dental kit. As a minimum, a small bottle of oil of cloves (eugenol) can serve as a topical toothache treatment or a tube of toothache gel can be obtained.

A fever thermometer should be included on trips.

People wearing contact lenses should carry the special suction cup or rubber pincer device to aid in their removal.

Do not forget mosquito netting and insect repellent if you are visiting the tropics or bug infested areas, particularly if insect borne disease is a possibility. The Extractor, as described on page 42, is recommended when travel is contemplated into areas where first aid care of snake bite or severe insect sting may be encountered.

Access to hydrogen peroxide, vinegar, alcohol and formalin may be useful when potential harm from jelly fish, coral, or ocean sponges is possible. Fishermen should carry a pair of side-cutting wire cutters, if fishing with barbed hooks, to facilitate their removal from human puncture wounds by the push-through-snip-off method.

To help you gather and organize your travel medical kit, the following outlines and quantities are provided in table format to match the text description of the non-prescription and recommended prescription components:

TABLE 6
THE TRAVEL MEDICAL KIT
NON-PRESCRIPTION COMPONENTS

QTY*	ITEM DESCRIPTION
1 ea	Spenco 2nd Skin Blister Kit
1 bottle	Potable Aqua—50 tablets
1 ea	Poly bottle—1 liter
1 ea	Hibiclens Surgical Scrub—4 oz
1 ea	Coverstrip—6/pack—$^{1}/_{2}$″ × 4″ strips
1 ea	Triple Antibiotic—1 oz tube
1 ea	Splinter Forceps
1 ea	#11 Scalpel Blade
10 pks	Q Tips—2/pack, sterile
1 roll	Tape, Waterproof—$^{1}/_{2}$″ wide
1 bottle	Actifed—24 tablets
1 ea	Bulb Syringe
1 bottle	Antacid Tablets—24 tablets
1 bottle	Meclizine 25 mg—10 tablets
1 bottle	Benadryl 25 mg—24 capsules
1 bottle	Mobigesic—24 tablets
1 tube	Hydrocortisone Cream .5%—1 oz
1 tube	Miconazole Cream 2%—1 oz
1 bottle	Diasorb—24 tablets
12 capsules	Imodium 2 mg

* Quantity recommended per individual traveler.

TABLE 7
THE TRAVEL MEDICAL KIT
RECOMMENDED PRESCRIPTION COMPONENTS

QTY*	ITEM DESCRIPTION
10 tablets	Doxycycline 100 mg
10 tablets	Bactrim DS
1 tube	Tobrex Ophthalmic Ointment .3%—1/8 oz
1 tube	Pontocaine Ophthalmic Ointment .5%—1/8 oz
1 tube	Topicort Ointment—1/2 oz
20+ tablets	Carafate 1 gram
20 tablets	Atarax 25 mg
24 tablets	Tylenol #3
1 box	Transderm Scop—4 patches ea

* Quantity recommended per individual traveler.

Assembling Your Medical Kit

The above kit, excluding prescription items, can be purchased pre-packed, and/or the individual items may be purchased separately from Indiana Camp Supply, Inc., PO Box 211, Hobart, Indiana 46342—telephone (219) 947-2525. Since 1972 Indiana Camp Supply has specialized in supporting wilderness expeditions and many governmental agencies with medical components. Besides the Travelers' Medical Kit recommended above, they carry an extensive listing of all manner of non-prescription medical articles available by mail order. *Wilderness Medicine, 3rd Edition* describes medical kit construction in detail for the problems of travel that extend beyond the requirements of the average foreign travel adventure.[3]

[3]*Wilderness Medicine, 3rd Edition*, is available from ICS Books, 107 East 89th Avenue, Merrillville, IN 46410, telephone (219) 769-0585, for $7.95 plus $1.50 shipping and handling.

Customizing Your Medical Kit

While this book offers basic suggestions for antibiotic and other medication, your physician advisors may wish to substitute other products. If alternate medications are to be used, fill in their names (brand name and generic), purpose, and dosage instructions in the following section. Special purpose items should also be obtained and included in the spaces provided.

Medications Recommended By My Doctor

The Customized Medical Kit
Purpose: Antibiotic
Qty:
Item: *Name, strength, and dosage instructions—*

Purpose: Alternate Antibiotic
Qty:
Item: *Name, strength, and dosage instructions—*

Purpose: Anti-diarrhea
Qty:
Item: *Name, strength, and dosage instructions—*

Purpose: Acute Mountain Sickness
Qty:
Item: *Name, strength, and dosage instructions—*

Purpose: Malaria Prophylaxis
Qty:
Item: *Name, strength, and dosage instructions—*

Purpose: Motion Sickness
Qty:
Item: *Name, strength, and dosage instructions—*

Purpose: Jet Lag
Qty:
Item: *Name, strength, and dosage instructions—*

Purpose: Water purification
Qty:
Item: *Name, strength, and dosage instructions—*

Purpose: Allergies
Qty:
Item: *Name, strength, and dosage instructions—*

Purpose: Pain Medication
Qty:
Item: *Name, strength, and dosage instructions—*

Purpose: Heart Burn/Gastritis
Qty:
Item: *Name, strength, and dosage instructions—*

Purpose: Cough/Cold Relief
Qty:
Item: *Name, strength, and dosage instructions—*

Chapter 9

Personal Information Section

Full Name _____

Street Address _____

City _____ **State** ____ **ZIP** _____

Telephone _____

Social Security Number _____

Passport Number _____

Birth Date _____**Place** _____

My Special Health Problems:
Include allergies, surgeries, current medical problems for which you routinely or occasionally take medication

Personal Prescription Medications:
Brand name, generic name, purpose, dosage instructions for each

Emergency Contacts at Home:
Names, addresses, telephones, relationship

Travel Medical Insurance:
Company, U.S. telephone, local country contact information, policy identification number

Names of Significant Other Traveling Companions
Names, home addresses, home telephones, relationship

Additional Family Member Information Page

Full Name _____

Social Security Number _____

Passport Number _____

Birth Date _____ **Place** _____

Special Health Problems:
Include allergies, surgeries, current medical problems for which you routinely or occasionally take medication

Personal Prescription Medications:
Brand name, generic name, purpose, dosage instructions for each

Travel Medical Insurance:
Policy identification number

Additional Family Member Information Page

Full Name _____

Social Security Number _____

Passport Number _____

Birth Date _____**Place** _____

Special Health Problems:
Include allergies, surgeries, current medical problems for which you routinely or occasionally take medication

Personal Prescription Medications:
Brand name, generic name, purpose, dosage instructions for each

Travel Medical Insurance:
Policy identification number

Additional Family Member Information Page

Full Name _____

Social Security Number _____

Passport Number _____

Birth Date _____ **Place** _____

Special Health Problems:
Include allergies, surgeries, current medical problems for which you routinely or occasionally take medication

Personal Prescription Medications:
Brand name, generic name, purpose, dosage instructions for each

Travel Medical Insurance:
Policy identification number

Additional Family Member Information Page

Full Name _____

Social Security Number _____

Passport Number _____

Birth Date _____ **Place** _____

Special Health Problems:
Include allergies, surgeries, current medical problems for which you routinely or occasionally take medication

Personal Prescription Medications:
Brand name, generic name, purpose, dosage instructions for each

Travel Medical Insurance:
Policy identification number

Country Information Page

Country:

Dates visit planned:

VISA requirements:

Immunizations required:

U.S. Embassy *addresses and telephone numbers: Refer to Travelers' Medical Resource, Country Information Database.*

IAMAT Physician *names, addresses, telephone numbers:*

Canadian High Commission *addresses and telephone numbers: Refer to Travelers' Medical Resource, Country Information Database.*

Business and other local contacts:

Country Information Page

Country:

Dates visit planned:

VISA requirements:

Immunizations required:

U.S. Embassy *addresses and telephone numbers: Refer to Travelers' Medical Resource, Country Information Database.*

IAMAT Physician *names, addresses, telephone numbers:*

Canadian High Commission *addresses and telephone numbers: Refer to Travelers' Medical Resource, Country Information Database.*

Business and other local contacts:

Country Information Page

Country:

Dates visit planned:

VISA requirements:

Immunizations required:

U.S. Embassy *addresses and telephone numbers: Refer to Travelers' Medical Resource, Country Information Database.*

IAMAT Physician *names, addresses, telephone numbers:*

Canadian High Commission *addresses and telephone numbers: Refer to Travelers' Medical Resource, Country Information Database.*

Business and other local contacts:

Country Information Page

Country:

Dates visit planned:

VISA requirements:

Immunizations required:

U.S. Embassy *addresses and telephone numbers: Refer to Travelers' Medical Resource, Country Information Database.*

IAMAT Physician *names, addresses, telephone numbers:*

Canadian High Commission *addresses and telephone numbers: Refer to Travelers' Medical Resource, Country Information Database.*

Business and other local contacts:

Country Information Page

Country:

Dates visit planned:

VISA requirements:

Immunizations required:

U.S. Embassy *addresses and telephone numbers: Refer to Travelers' Medical Resource, Country Information Database.*

IAMAT Physician *names, addresses, telephone numbers:*

Canadian High Commission *addresses and telephone numbers: Refer to Travelers' Medical Resource, Country Information Database.*

Business and other local contacts:

Country Information Page

Country:

Dates visit planned:

VISA requirements:

Immunizations required:

U.S. Embassy *addresses and telephone numbers: Refer to Travelers' Medical Resource, Country Information Database.*

IAMAT Physician *names, addresses, telephone numbers:*

Canadian High Commission *addresses and telephone numbers: Refer to Travelers' Medical Resource, Country Information Database.*

Business and other local contacts:

Country Information Page

Country:

Dates visit planned:

VISA requirements:

Immunizations required:

U.S. Embassy *addresses and telephone numbers: Refer to Travelers' Medical Resource, Country Information Database.*

IAMAT Physician *names, addresses, telephone numbers:*

Canadian High Commission *addresses and telephone numbers: Refer to Travelers' Medical Resource, Country Information Database.*

Business and other local contacts:

Country Information Page

Country:

Dates visit planned:

VISA requirements:

Immunizations required:

U.S. Embassy *addresses and telephone numbers: Refer to Travelers' Medical Resource, Country Information Database.*

IAMAT Physician *names, addresses, telephone numbers:*

Canadian High Commission *addresses and telephone numbers: Refer to Travelers' Medical Resource, Country Information Database.*

Business and other local contacts:

Country Information Page

Country:

Dates visit planned:

VISA requirements:

Immunizations required:

U.S. Embassy *addresses and telephone numbers: Refer to Travelers' Medical Resource, Country Information Database.*

IAMAT Physician *names, addresses, telephone numbers:*

Canadian High Commission *addresses and telephone numbers: Refer to Travelers' Medical Resource, Country Information Database.*

Business and other local contacts:

Country Information Page

Country:

Dates visit planned:

VISA requirements:

Immunizations required:

U.S. Embassy *addresses and telephone numbers:*
Refer to Travelers' Medical Resource, Country Information Database.

IAMAT Physician *names, addresses, telephone numbers:*

Canadian High Commission *addresses and telephone numbers:*
Refer to Travelers' Medical Resource, Country Information Database.

Business and other local contacts:

Country Information Page

Country:

Dates visit planned:

VISA requirements:

Immunizations required:

U.S. Embassy *addresses and telephone numbers: Refer to Travelers' Medical Resource, Country Information Database.*

IAMAT Physician *names, addresses, telephone numbers:*

Canadian High Commission *addresses and telephone numbers: Refer to Travelers' Medical Resource, Country Information Database.*

Business and other local contacts:

INDEX